BARGELLO AND RELATED STITCHERY

BARGELLO
and
RELATED STITCHERY

By CHARLES BARNES and DAVID P. BLAKE

HEARTHSIDE PRESS, INC.
GREAT NECK, NEW YORK 11021

Photography by Joseph Ratke

Contents

OUR GRATEFUL ACKNOWLEDGMENTS TO:

Mrs. Nedda Anders, without whose persistent and invaluable assistance this book would never have been possible;

Mr. Arthur McGee, for his initial encouragement and boundless enthusiasm;

Mrs. Sybil Christopher, for her gracious and generous spirit;

Mr. Rod Keefer, for his many years of unselfish friendship and inspiration;

Mrs. Jean Simmons and Mrs. Hazel Burns for their constant support and many hours of selfless stitching;

Mr. Ron Wentz, for his loyalty and devoted service;

Mrs. Rena Sherman, for her marvelous common sense and vast knowledge of needlework, which she so generously shared;

Mrs. John Sturges, Mrs. Elain Wolfson, Mrs. Brock Peters, and many, many more clients for their years of patronage, good advice, and the faith that they placed in our work;

and our special thanks to *WRMB,* for just being *WRMB.*

Charles Barnes
David P. Blake

SPRING 1971

BARGELLO AND RELATED STITCHERY

Introduction

The origins of Bargello needlepoint appear to be lost in history. Confusing and conflicting stories abound as to its ethnic origin, its time of origin and the reason for its origin. All of these discrepancies are further complicated by the variety of names applied to the stitches. They are called Bargello, Florentine, Hungarian, Flame, Brick, Byzantine, Old Florentine, and many, many other names. Early examples have been found in Germany, France, Austria, Italy, England, Hungary and other Northern European countries. It would seem logical that, as artisans experimented with needle, thread and canvas, the same basic geometric patterns would have been developed by each, through trial and error. It is of course true that, in many instances, a particular arrangement of colors and stitch patterns may have been associated with a region or group of people. However, as anyone who has experimented with needle and thread has found, just when you have "discovered" a new stitch, you find that someone has been there years, perhaps centuries, before you.

The name Bargello appears to have become associated with a specific pattern, examples of which can be seen on a set of chairs presently in the Museo Nazionale in Florence. This building served for many years as a prison, and was known as The Bargello. The Bargello was transformed into the Museo Nazionale in 1857. It was not until 1886 that the chairs were acquired by the museum. Thus, their relationship to the former prison and its name, The Bargello, remains one of the inexplicable questions of history.

For the purpose of this book, the name Bargello will be considered all-inclusive, and will cover various patterns and stitch arrangements as types of Bargello needlepoint. This decision is made in the light of the fact that for several generations Bargello has been considered, and used, as the one all-inclusive name that best characterizes the various stitch arrangements. The names Hungarian, Flame, Florentine, Brick, etc. are really much more restrictive since they usually refer to a specific stitch or color arrangement. The basic characteristics of Bargello needlepoint seem to be:

1. The stitches are upright on the canvas, or at least parallel to the threads of the canvas. Most needlepoint stitches are worked diagonally and cover both the warp and woof threads of canvas. Bargello stitches cover

only the warp, or only the woof, threads of canvas. The remaining canvas threads are covered by the thickness of the yarn. The yarn merely spreads out and covers the thread.

2. Stitches are usually worked over the same number of threads throughout one piece of needlepoint.

3. Stitches frequently encroach upon the next, most often by half of the number of threads of the previous stitch. That is, if the first stitch covers four threads of canvas, and the second stitch covers four threads of canvas, the two stitches will share two threads of canvas in common. The second stitch will be two threads above or below the previous stitch. This overlapping of adjoining stitches by one-half of the previous stitch results in many of the basic geometric, diamond and serrated patterns. Many diamond and serrated patterns may be formed by overlapping adjoining stitches by *odd* numbers of canvas threads. This usually results in higher peaks and valleys than would have resulted if the stitches had overlapped by one-half.

4. Colors are usually worked in numerous shades, progressing from light to dark, or vice versa. This results in a variation of color, usually associated with the Flame stitch. This sequence of shades and colors is frequently repeated over and over until the entire piece of canvas is filled with the same progression of shades and colors.

5. Most of the patterns are built upon one row of stitches. Once the first row has been counted out, all the remaining rows follow the same stitch pattern and are simply built upon this base row of stitches. With this type of pattern, once the base row has been established, the hard work is usually accomplished. The balance of the canvas is filled in with rows, each following the preceeding row. All that is necessary is to make sure that each stitch picks up the same number of canvas threads. Brocaded effects result when the size of adjoining stitches in one row are varied. Each succeeding row continues this pattern of stitches of varied length.

6. The canvas most usually used is a mono, or single thread canvas. A double thread canvas tends to push the stitches further apart, thereby allowing the canvas itself to show through. Specific projects in this book have been worked on a double thread canvas for the purpose of adding variety and to give examples of what can be accomplished by using unorthodox materials.

The purpose of Bargello needlepoint, as with most crafts, is to produce something beautiful and useful. Of equal importance is the fact that it should be enjoyable and give satisfaction to the person engaged in the project. With this in mind, the various projects in this book were worked out to allow for a wide range of uses, materials, and techniques. They were designed both as an end in themselves and as a source of inspiration to the needlepointer. A pattern used for an eyeglass case could, just as well, with experimentation and imagination, become a room-size rug. By all means, experiment. Try different color combinations. Work out various stitch patterns. But above everything else, enjoy Bargello.

I Materials

THE CANVAS

Canvas is the evenly woven fabric which serves as the basis for the needle-point stitches. The yarn is placed over the threads of the canvas in specific patterns. This arrangement of the yarn results in the various stitches known to needlepoint. The canvas can be divided into two basic categories, that is, single thread and double thread.

PENELOPE CANVAS

The double thread canvas is referred to as Penelope canvas. Stitches are generally worked over two vertical and two horizontal threads of canvas. The vertical threads are the warp threads. The horizontal threads are the woof threads. The warp threads are, in the finer size canvas, woven very closely together. In some of the finest canvases, the two warp threads are side by side and function as a single thread. With large-size rug canvas, it sometimes becomes difficult to determine which is the warp and which is the woof thread since they are both spaced equal distance apart. In this case, an arbitrary decision is made as to which two threads will become the warp pair and which two threads will become the woof pair. Once this decision is made, it should be adhered to consistently. Most instructions consider the pair of warp threads as one thread, and the pair of woof threads as one thread. With this in mind, remember that if instructions direct that a stitch be placed across two threads on a Penelope canvas, the stitch will in actuality be placed across the two *pair* of threads, or four threads. The accepted practice is to place the warp threads vertically when working on the canvas. However, in some of the projects in this book, the canvas has been deliber-ately turned so that the reverse is true. This places the stitches closer to-gether, and gives a fuller, more luxurious texture than if the stitches were worked on the canvas in the conventional manner. Penelope canvas is frequently tan or olive in color. Some of the newer brands are white. The color has little relevance to the finished design unless the project incorporates a great many light shades. Then a light-colored canvas is to be preferred. The white canvas is perhaps the easiest to work with since the threads are more easily visible. White canvas is also preferred if designs are to be marked directly on the canvas before the needlepoint is begun.

Mono-Canvas

Single thread canvas is commonly known as mono-canvas. It is also called French mono-canvas, unimesh, congress canvas, or uni-canvas. The basic difference between the mono-canvas and the Penelope canvas is that there is no distinction made between the warp and woof threads. Each thread is the same size in diameter, and all threads are spaced the same distance apart. The mono-canvas is almost universally white in color. The smaller sizes may be tan or olive. The white seems to be the most popular and easiest on the eyes.

Size of Canvas

Canvas size is referred to as being of a certain size mesh. The mesh size refers to the number of threads per linear inch. A canvas which contains 10 threads to the inch would be considered 10 mesh; 14 threads to the inch would be considered 14 mesh. The pair of warp and woof threads in Penelope canvas is considered a single thread. Thus, 10 mesh Penelope canvas will in actuality contain 10 pair, or 20 threads, per linear inch. Canvas ranges from 40 threads to the inch to 3 threads to the inch. The finer mesh canvases are primarily used for petit point, while the largest mesh is used for rugs. The most popular mesh sizes are 14, 12, 10, 5 and 4. Projects in this book have been worked on a variety of meshes ranging from 16 to 5 mesh. This will enable you to have some idea of the type of designs suitable to each mesh, and to see the texture which results. When choosing the size mesh for a design, one should consider the ultimate use of the finished canvas. The smaller the project, the smaller the mesh (and the higher the canvas number). For book covers, book markers, headbands and other similar projects, the smaller mesh canvas will allow for more development of pattern within the small confines of size. Pillows, vests, rugs and other larger projects will take more to the larger canvas since the pattern will be best seen if it is large and bold. Also, the larger the mesh, the fewer stitches required to cover a given area. With a 5 mesh canvas it may require only 25 stitches to cover one square inch. With a 14 mesh canvas, it may require as many as 196 stitches to cover the same square inch.

PIECING CANVAS

Canvas is available in widths ranging from 18 inches to as wide as 54 inches. The most common widths are 36 and 42 inches. Whenever possible, make sure that the canvas is wide enough for the finished project. This will avoid the necessity of piecing together strips of canvas, either before needlepointing or after the needlepoint is completed. If pieces of canvas are to be joined, it is best to accomplish this before the project is begun. Simply overlay the two strips of canvas by several inches. Align the threads of the canvas so that they match. It may be necessary to stitch them together every several inches before beginning. The needlepoint is worked through both layers. All projects in this book can be accommodated on canvas 42 inches wide.

SELECTING CANVAS

Since the canvas will be the basis of any project, be sure that it is of excellent quality. The canvas will have to stand a great deal of wear and tear while it is being worked on, during the blocking process, and of course, when the finished needlepoint is put to use. If the canvas appears to be coated with a loose powder do not use it. The threads are of inferior quality and have been heavily treated with sizing. Once the sizing is removed, either through the blocking process or cleaning, the canvas will have no body. If the individual threads of canvas can easily be broken by hand it probably will not be strong enough to stand much blocking or wear. Also avoid canvas which appears to be woven unevenly. If the canvas is uneven, certainly there is no way that the finished stitches will be even. This also applies to canvas which has been stretched out of shape. Canvas threads which have knots in them will only present a problem later. Either the needlepoint will not cover the knots, or the knots will come undone during the blocking process or when the piece is put to use.

Allowing Margins

Before working on the canvas, make sure that you have allowed sufficient margins on all sides. These margins will be necessary for the blocking and when the needlepoint is mounted. For small projects, allow at least 1 to 1½ inch margins. The larger projects will need at least 2 inches, and more if possible. The canvas threads can be unravelled until there is no canvas left upon which to work. To prevent this from happening, the edges of the canvas must be prepared by one of several methods. The most common is to cover the edges with masking tape. This not only prevents the threads from unravelling, but also keeps the yarn from becoming ensnared in the edges of the canvas as you work. The edges may also be turned under ¼ to ½ inch and stitched in place, either by hand or by machine. This latter method is the most secure. (Tape sometimes is pulled free, carrying with it several threads of the canvas). The stitched edge also gives a firmer margin to be used when blocking. If the project is of such a size that you find it difficult to hold it flat while working on it, the best solution is to roll the canvas, leaving the portion to be worked on exposed. The ends of the rolls can be secured with pins. By all means, avoid crumpling the canvas up in your hands as you work. It makes a mess of the canvas and the stitches will not be placed evenly. If it still is a problem to hold the canvas rolled as you work, then resort to the use of a frame. The canvas will be held taut and your hands will be free to work as you please. Do not try to save a few pennies on the canvas. The project will involve a considerable investment in time and further materials. This investment should not be jeopardized by the selection of an inferior canvas.

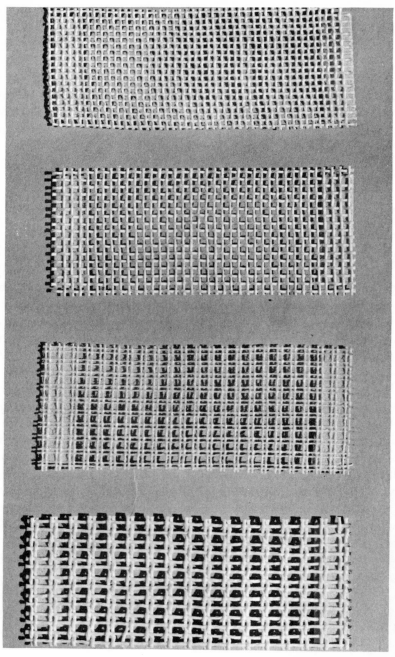

1. *Canvas (top to bottom)* 14 *mesh mono;* 10 *mesh mono;* 7 *mesh Penelope;* 5 *mesh Penelope*

THE NEEDLES

Tapestry and rug needles are used exclusively for the projects in this book. The tapestry needles range in sizes from 24 to 16. They are distinguished from ordinary needles in that they have a blunt point and an elongated eye. The blunt point is designed to prevent the needle from splitting the canvas threads as you work. Also, since the needle is going through the holes in the canvas, there is no need for the needle to have a sharp point. The elongated eye is necessary to accommodate the relatively large size of the yarns used in needlepoint and rugs. The larger the number the smaller the needle, and the smaller the number the larger the needle. The correct choice of the size of the needle to be used with a specific project will be determined by the size of canvas, the size of the yarn, and by personal preference. The needle should be small enough that it passes easily through the canvas. On the other hand, it must be large enough to be threaded easily with the yarn used. If it is too small to handle the yarn, not only will your patience fray every time the needle is threaded, but the yarn itself will become frayed. Finally, since every hand is different, you may decide for yourself just which of several needles feels comfortable and allows you to work smoothly and efficiently. Tapestry needles are usually available in a package of varying sizes. It is advisable to have several packages available. They can be stored in plastic pill bottles.

Rug needles are not as readily available as tapestry needles. They also have blunt points and a very large elongated eye. It is best to purchase several of each size when you find them available since they can be very difficult to find, and there is no adequate substitute.

While working on a specific piece of needlepoint, it will be convenient if you thread a needle with each color used in the design. This will save considerable time in threading and rethreading every time you switch from one color to another. It would be helpful to arrange the threaded needles in the sequence of colors on a large pincushion. This way you will be less likely to pick up the wrong color as you move from one portion of the design to another.

THE YARNS

A wide selection of yarns, both traditional and novelty, have been used in the projects in this book. Needlepoint is traditionally worked in tapestry wool or Persian (crewel) wool. However, there are many new, and not so new, yarns which produce admirable results, and there is no reason why they should be excluded from the list of acceptable yarns. The fact that certain yarns have been traditional is not a sufficient reason to limit ourselves in the creation of beautiful and useful projects.

When selecting a yarn, there are certain principles which should guide you. The first, and probably the most basic is, what is available? Not everyone has access to a large selection of Persian or tapestry wool. The second consideration should be the amount of wear the finished project will receive. Certain yarns will stand much more wear than others. The third consideration will be the finished effect that is desired. Since each yarn works up differently and produces a different texture and sheen, this, too, should be taken into account. If a traditional effect is desired, then the traditional materials should be used. If a bolder and more modern effect is desired, then consider more unorthodox materials. Of course, some consideration should be given to costs involved. Persian wool can be very expensive, especially for larger projects. If costs are a problem, substitute a less expensive yarn.

PERSIAN WOOL

This wool is generally available in 3-thread strands. It is perhaps the most practical, longest wearing and best all-around wool. The three threads can be separated or combined, to give an almost unlimited selection of weight and colors. Because of this fact, it can be used on almost any size canvas. If instructions call for a 4-ply Persian wool, it is best to thread the needle with 2-ply and use the yarn double rather than use 4-ply in the needle. The use of 4-ply would cause considerable bulk in the eye of the needle. When they are doubled over you would have 8-ply of yarn going through the canvas every time. The range of colors available will meet every need. Since most colors are available in from 5 to 7 shades, they are exceptionally suited to the shadings required by certain patterns. While some stores offer it only by the 4-ounce skein, many stores offer it by the ounce, or by the strand. This makes it convenient and, to an extent, economical to buy since you may purchase as little as one strand. Where it would be necessary to buy an entire skein of other types of yarn to gain one additional color, with Persian yarn you may buy only the number of strands of yarn necessary for that color. Persian yarn is usually mothproofed, and of exceptional wearing quality. It is preferred above most other yarns.

TAPESTRY YARN

This yarn is usually available in any needlework shop or the needlework department of major department stores. It is generally available in 40-yard skeins. It, too, is a tough, long-wearing yarn. Because of its tight twist and long fibers, it is particularly easy to use on needlepoint canvas. It is less versatile than the Persian yarn because it cannot be used on as many different mesh canvases. Its tight twist prevents it from being easily separated for the finer canvas. If it is used double, considerable care has to be exercised that the two threads of yarn lie side by side. If they become twisted the result is a very uneven stitch. The color range is also much more limited. It has been manufactured as a background wool for many of the needlepoint pieces that are sold in department stores with the design already worked.

KNITTING YARN

The chief blessing of knitting yarn is that is readily available in every town, village and hamlet. It comes in a relatively large selection of colors. It is also very inexpensive. The yarn can be worked either single, as it comes from the skein, or double to cover larger mesh canvas. When using knitting yarn, extreme care must be taken not to pull the yarn tight. There is a great deal of elasticity in knitting yarn, and if it is pulled tight while needlepointing, the canvas may be pulled completely out of shape. No amount of blocking will return the canvas to its original shape. If it can be blocked straight, the yarn may eventually pull the canvas back to its crooked shape. The other major disadvantage is that it has a tendency to pill, much like a knitted sweater. Even taking these two disadvantages into account, there are many projects which can utilize this greatly overlooked yarn.

MOHAIR YARN

Another ignored yarn is mohair. Greatly used in knitting and crocheting, it can produce very unusual and highly serviceable projects. It has very little elasticity, and of course, the yarn presents no particular problem as far as pilling goes. While the color range is somewhat limited, the blending of the fuzzy stitches achieved in the finished product creates an interesting blend of colors. The yarn can be used singly, or in multiple strands. Because of the nature of the yarn, individual strands may be combined and will blend together as one piece of yarn. The colors can thus be blended as you wish. Initially you may experience some difficulty in handling the yarn, but with perseverence this difficulty can be overcome. While working with the mohair yarn, the fuzzy ends of the yarn will become trapped in the canvas in the adjoining stitches. After blocking, the yarn may be brushed vigorously to loosen the trapped ends. The brushing should be across the stitches for best effect. Mohair yarn is generally more expensive than knitting yarn, so some consideration should be given to the amount of yarn required.

DMC No. 5 Cotton Perle

This yarn's chief advantage is its range of very bright, highly glossy colors. It can be used only on small mesh canvas. It has very little softness and therefore cannot be combined into more than one ply very easily. If used as a double ply, care must be exercised that the two strands of yarn lie side by side and do not become twisted. Otherwise a very uneven stitch will result. The yarn is particularly suited to bright accent points. It is most effective when used beside a dull, soft yarn. The soft yarn serves to accent the brilliance and sheen of the DMC. It is not recommended if the project is to receive a great deal of wear and tear. The skeins contain about 27 yards of yarn.

Paternayan Rug Yarn

What the Persian yarn is to the needlepoint yarns, the Paternayan Rug yarn is to all rug yarns. It also comes in as wide a range of colors as the Persian yarns. It has a fine, tight twist which results in an especially long-wearing project. Most stores sell the rug yarn in one-pound lots only, and many only on special order. However, some stores will sell the 4-ounce skeins. For large projects, and most rugs, it is the yarn to use for long wearing results.

Cotton and Rayon Rug Yarn

The chief advantage of this yarn is that it is readily available and very inexpensive. However, since it does not wear as well as the wool rug yarn, its use is very limited. The color range is restricted to the basic primary colors, and in most instances there is no variation of shading. For projects not subject to wear, it can be used as an accent yarn. It has considerable sheen and is therefore effective when combined with a dull surfaced wool yarn. Most brands claim to be colorfast, and washable. This may be important in some projects.

Other Yarns

Various other silk, rayon or other synthetic yarns are also available. When substituting, be sure to take into consideration the yarn's serviceability, future availability, and its suitability to needlepoint projects.

Dye Lots

When selecting the yarn to be used in a given project, some consideration should be given to the dye lot. While many manufacturers state that dye lots are always matched, in most cases there are some variations in shading between different lots. Therefore, try to estimate the amount of yarn required, and either buy this quantity outright, or lay away enough for the entire job.

Length of Yarns

The length of yarn in the needle should be about 18 inches. If you are using the yarn double in the needle, then a longer strand may be used. If the strand of yarn is too long it will continually tangle as you work. Also, the friction of the canvas on the yarn tends to remove some of the yarn fibers. If the yarn strand is too long, you will actually wear out one end of the yarn as it passes back and forth through the canvas. The friction also causes the yarn to come untwisted as you work. Therefore, try to maintain the same twist on the yarn as the strand is used.

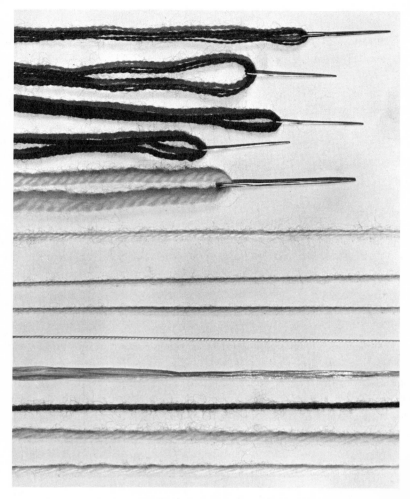

2. *Threaded needles (top to bottom) No. 18 tapestry needle threaded with 4-ply Persian yarn; No. 18 tapestry needle with 6-ply Persian yarn; No. 18 tapestry needle, double strand of tapestry yarn; No. 18 tapestry needle with double strand of knitting yarn; Rug needle, double strand of Paternayan rug yarn. Yarns: 2 strands of Mohair; Tapestry; Knitting; DMC No. 5 Perle; Synthetic Straw; 3-ply Persian; Paternayan rug yarn; Cotton and Rayon rug yarn.*

Beginning and Ending Yarn

With many-ply yarn some difficulty may be encountered in threading the needle. Turn back about two inches of yarn and press between the thumb and forefinger. Keep the loop formed well down between the thumb and forefinger. Pressing the yarn tightly together, slip the eye of the needle over the loop. If you have repeated difficulty, the eye of the needle may be too small for the type of yarn you are using. To begin, run the yarn through several mesh of the canvas outside the area to be needlepointed. Run the yarn across the back of the canvas for several inches so that when you begin needlepointing the stitches will catch this strand of yarn and secure it to the back of the finished canvas. Do not use knots. They will cause bumps on the surface of the needlepoint. These bumps will show through and cause the needlepoint to wear unevenly eventually. To finish a piece of yarn, weave the yarn through the back of several of the stitches. Do not end many pieces of yarn in the same place or the yarn ends will cause bumps. All ends of yarn should be clipped very close to the back of the finished needlepoint. This should be done as you finish a piece of yarn. If long ends of yarn are left hanging from the back they will become tangled in the stitches, and the ends may pull through to the face of the needlepoint.

Fig. 1 Holding the needle

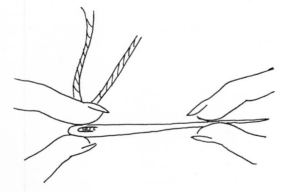

II Techniques

ADAPTING DESIGNS

There are two basic methods of adapting the size of a design. The first has to do with designs which are drawn directly on the canvas, with little thought given to the exact length and placement of the stitches. These would include such designs as the Unicorn, Etherea and Hector the Lion. Here the stitches are worked into the outlines of the design itself. The second has to do with patterns which require a definite placement of stitches and color to achieve the finished design. These would include such designs as the Shaded Square Pillow, Arabesque Bracelet, Rose Belt and other counted designs.

METHOD 1

The first method requires freehand drawing. A given area of the original design is copied into comparable areas of the enlarged or reduced design. Assuming you wish to enlarge a given design, the small design is marked off into squares or rectangles. In order to enlarge the design, it will be necessary to draw the same number of squares or rectangles on a piece of paper the size you wish the enlarged design to be. The squares and rectangles have to be placed in the same proportion as those on the small design. If the finished size is to be four times as large as the small original design, each square or rectangle should be four times as large as the squares or rectangles on the original design. In some cases, the scale of the projects in this book has been noted for your convenience. You will see that each square equals a given number of inches on the finished design. Simply draw these squares as indicated, placing them in the same sequence as the original design. The portion of the original design that is in the upper left-hand corner is then drawn in the upper left-hand corner of the enlarged design. The portion of the original design that is in the square directly below is transferred to the square directly below the first square. This procedure is repeated until the entire design has been copied, square for square on the enlarged design.

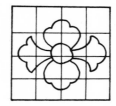

Fig. 2 You can enlarge or reduce a design by dividing it into four or more equal sections (method 1). Rule lines, the same distance apart, horizontally and vertically to make squares. This sketch has 16 squares, so divide a piece of paper the size of the design you want into 16 squares. Draw in the pattern, following the lines from square to square.

Graph Paper Transfer

Once the design has been enlarged or reduced there are two procedures for transferring it to the canvas. Perhaps the most accurate, albeit time-consuming method, is the use of graph paper. Any errors in the design may be corrected on the paper before the design is begun on the canvas. However, once the design has been worked on the graph paper, each stitch has to be counted and transferred, one by one, to the canvas itself. This requires a great deal of accuracy, patience and time. First, decide what mesh canvas you will be using. Then secure graph paper of the same number of lines per inch. Transfer the design from the enlarged paper directly onto the graph paper. The graph lines now become equal to the threads of the canvas. Using colored pencils, draw individual stitches on the graph paper representing the colors of the finished design. These colors would only approximate the colors of the yarns to be used. An exact match of colors would be next to impossible. Once the stitches have been drawn in the design on the graph paper, you are ready to begin on the canvas. Starting at some convenient point of departure on the design; the center, left hand corner, bottom center, etc., copy the stitches you have drawn on the graph paper using the needle and yarn on the canvas. You will see that each stitch or group of stitches have to first be counted on the graph paper. Then you have to find the comparable position on the canvas and count out the stitches again as you work them. Then it is necessary to return to the graph paper for another stitch or group of stitches. Back to the canvas again. This process continues until the entire design has been transferred, stitch by stitch. While it is very time-consuming, it is also very accurate.

Direct Tracing Transfer

The second, and quicker procedure is to transfer the design from the paper directly onto the canvas. Once the design has been enlarged and traced on the paper, the pattern and general details of the design should be outlined in heavy black lines. The stitches are then worked directly on the canvas using the outline of the design as a guide. With this method, errors have to be corrected as they occur on the canvas. This may require a great deal of ripping out of stitches. With care it can be handled successfully and save a great deal of time. Whatever is used in marking the design on the paper, or on the canvas itself *must* be waterproof. When blocking the canvas, or when it has to be cleaned, any impermanent marking material may run and permanently stain the canvas and finished needlepoint. Of great help here are permanent, waterproof felt tip markers. You must be certain that they are permanent and waterproof before using. If in doubt, mark a small scrap of canvas. Immerse in water and allow to dry. If the ink runs or discolors the water, avoid using it. Oil base paints, or permanent acrylic paints may also be used. Once the design has been darkened, place the canvas directly over the design itself. You will see the heavy lines of the design showing through the holes of the canvas. Using your choice of waterproof materials, trace the design directly onto the canvas itself. Tape, or otherwise secure the canvas over the design so that it does not shift as you work. Also check to see that the threads of the canvas are running horizontal and vertical to the original design. Once the outline has been transferred, the entire design may be painted in with waterproof materials. Do not try to match exactly the colors of the yarns to be used. The painted design is only a guide for your needlepoint stitches. If paints are used, they should be thinned to about the consistency of milk. Apply them sparingly with a fine brush. They should not clog the holes of the canvas, nor should they run through to the reverse side of the canvas.

If you feel that the colors should be changed once you begin to work on the canvas, do not hesitate to substitute different colors. You will run into a problem only when trying to cover a dark area with light colors. In this case it would be better to repaint that area before beginning the needlepoint. Whatever the material used to mark the canvas, be sure that it is thoroughly dry before beginning the needlepoint. In the case of oil base paints, this may require a wait of several days, or even a week, before the canvas is ready.

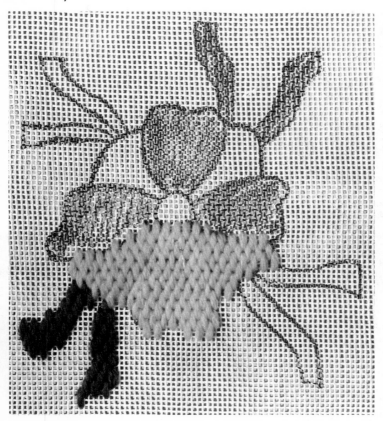

3. *The design on the canvas, partially outlined with permanent felt tip pens, and partially painted. The outlined or painted area serves only as a guide to the placement of stitches. Because of the length of the stitches, the needlepointed area will hardly ever be confined exactly to the outlined area.*

Method 2

The second method of adapting a design requires the use of graph paper or actual canvas to accomplish. If you wish the design to be larger than the original, you may do several things. Each stitch may be repeated, both horizontally and vertically. Each stitch may be lengthened. Or the design may be transferred to a comparably larger canvas. If the design is to be made smaller, the stitches may be shortened. Since the proportion of the design will vary as the number of stitches, or length of stitches is varied, the design should first be worked out on graph paper or on the canvas itself. Any adjustments necessary to correct changes in the design proportion can be accomplished at this time.

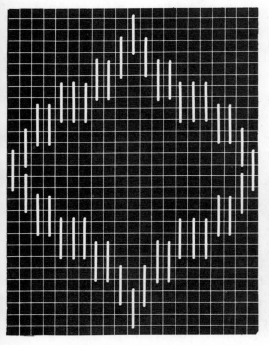

Fig. 3 Altering designs. Basic design worked on 10 and 12 mesh mono canvas. Each stitch covers 4 threads of canvas.

Fig. 4 Altering designs. Design worked on 12 mesh mono canvas. Each stitch has been shortened to cover only 2 threads of canvas. The same number and sequence of stitches have been retained as in the basic design.

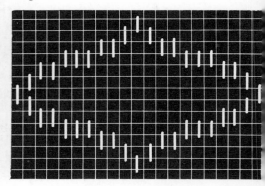

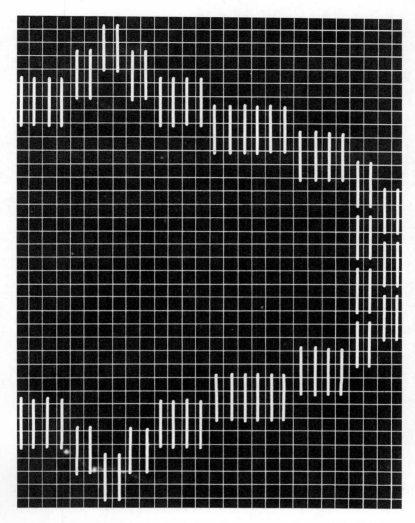

Fig. 5 Altering designs. Design worked on 12 mesh mono canvas. Each stitch has been worked over 4 threads of canvas. The number of stitches has been doubled across the design.

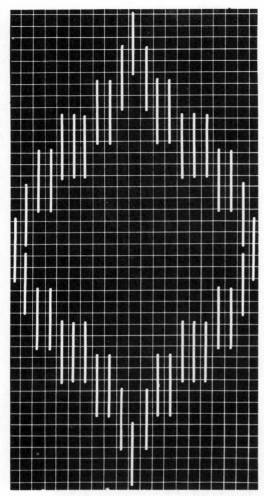

Fig. 6 Altering designs. Design worked on 12 mesh mono canvas. Each stitch has been lengthened to cover 6 threads of canvas. The same number and sequence of stitches have been retained as in the basic design.

4. *Basic design*

5. *Larger canvas*

6. *Shortened stitches*

7. *Repeated stitches*

8. *Lengthened stitches*

THE SAMPLER

The importance of a sampler cannot be overestimated. With it all manner of problems can be solved, either before they present themselves, or after they are encountered. While the investment of time and material may seem to be a waste, it should also be noted that a few cents worth of canvas and yarn, and a few minutes time expended on the sampler may save many, many hours of frustration, and many dollars in materials wasted. For most purposes, a small square or strip of canvas, (often excess from a previous project) can be utilized as a sampler. Rather than use a number of miniscule scraps for samplers, use one piece of sufficient size to allow you to experiment with various stitch and color placements, side by side, so that their effect can be easily determined.

1. Since the colors and textures of the yarn vary considerably, it is impossible to determine the effects they will have upon one another until they are worked out on canvas. The intensity of a color is determined by the quantity of light it reflects. While a skein of yarn may look overly brillant while lying on a table top, it must be remembered that when worked up into the canvas, there will only be a fraction of an inch of that same yarn to reflect the light. Thus, the colors will tend to become more subdued when worked up. Also the interaction of various colors cannot truly be determined until they are worked in the canvas, side by side, in the same proportion as they will have in the finished design. Therefore, it is advisable to take the colors and yarns to be used, and work a small portion of the design to see if that is what you had in mind before beginning.

2. Often the weight of the yarn varies from color to color, or from batch to batch. If the yarn is not sufficiently full, the canvas threads will not be covered. Rather than work a portion of the finished canvas only to find that the canvas is showing through, it is better to try the yarns on the sampler. If the sampler canvas shows through, there is no harm. If the canvas on the finished needlepoint shows through, you have to either live with it, add additional stitches over the previous stitches, or rip out all the stitches and begin again. If additional stitches are added, they must be added with extreme care or they will be obvious. It is very difficult to make the added ply of yarn appear as part of the original stitches. If the stitches are ripped out, the canvas holes will undoubtedly be stretched larger

than their original size. This defect is very difficult to correct. If you find, on the sampler, that the canvas shows through, use additional ply of yarn, or switch to finer mesh canvas.

3. Often it is necessary to estimate the amount of yarn required to cover a given area of canvas. Since every needleworker uses different quantities of yarn, depending on the tension applied and the method of stitching, there is no formula that can be established once and for all. To gain some approximation of the yarn required, determine the amount of yarn it takes to cover a given area, or to complete one motif. Secondly, determine the size of the canvas to be covered, or the number of motifs to be used. You will then be able to approximate the amount of yarn you will need. For example, if it takes 10 strands to cover 4 square inches, or to complete one motif, and the finished project is 10 inches by 10 inches, or requires 25 motifs, you will need 250 strands to cover the entire area. Once this figure has been arrived at, you will know how much yarn to buy so that you will not run short, nor will you have an excess of yarn when completed.

4. A pattern may have quite a different look when worked on a different size canvas. The only safe method of determining how the pattern will look when worked up, is to work a small portion of the design on the required canvas. Rather than start a project and find that the scale of the design is too large or too small, it is better to try the design and make the necessary corrections, if needed, before the actual canvas is started. This also applies to designs which are enlarged or reduced by altering the number or length of stitches.

5. A sampler can be an invaluable source of reference. A particular color combination, or pattern of stitches may be forgotten. Rather than have to rely solely on memory for these things, it is much better to have the stitches and colors at your fingertips. In addition to preserving the good combinations, the bad combinations and mistakes are also there so that the same errors are not repeated. The sampler can give an idea of the length of time required to complete a project. By working a specific area and comparing that to the total area involved, an estimate of the time can be made.

Many people still feel that the sampler is a waste unless it is put to a constructive use. If this is your thinking, when there is a little space left on the canvas, fill in the background with suitable stitches and colors, and make the sampler up into a belt, pillow, footstool top, or other useful article. Frequently the contrasts of the colors and stitches produce results of great charm and spontaneity.

9. *A sampler incorporating a variety of Bargello and other needlepoint stitches. With such a sampler, stitches can be learned, color combinations tried, and various stitch combinations practiced without wasting time and materials on the finished projects. Courtesy Mrs. Rena Sherman.*

FRAMES

Frames can be one of the most valuable and useful adjuncts to Bargello. If you are accustomed to doing needlepoint without a frame, it would serve you well to consider the benefits and, if necessary, to re-learn needle-pointing on a frame. The basic principle of the needlepoint in any form is that the stitches are placed over regularly spaced canvas threads. As the canvas is handled, the threads lose some of their original regularity. In many cases the stitches themselves pull the canvas out of shape. As the canvas becomes progressively filled, it also becomes progressively crooked. The stitches worked on the canvas at the beginning are placed over canvas which is fresh and regularly spaced. As the work continues, the stitches are placed over canvas which becomes more and more out of line. Then one has to depend upon blocking to pull both the canvas and stitches back into their proper alignment. With the use of the frame, the canvas retains its original regularity and the last stitch will be as straight as the first. Frequently the whole process of blocking becomes unnecessary. This eliminates a great deal of wear and tear on both the canvas and the person doing the blocking. In many instances, the stitches may succeed in pulling the canvas so completely out of shape that it may never be returned to its original shape, or if it is, the stitches may eventually cause the canvas to go crooked after the piece has been finished and mounted. In the case of rugs or other larger pieces, a frame is essential since it is almost impossible to hold the canvas in hand as it is being worked on. The size of the project may prevent you from working on the center of the canvas. If heavy yarns are used, the weight of the worked area may become uncomfortable. For all of these problems, the frame is the answer. There are several types of frames, each designed for specific projects.

EMBROIDERY FRAMES

The smallest, and most common, are the circular hoops used in embroidery. They are limited in their use with needlepoint however. The thickness of the canvas, particularly when covered with stitches, makes it almost impossible to keep the two hoops together. Even the types with the adjustable screws do not seem to hold the canvas adequately. Again, when the canvas is placed over the bottom hoop, it is forced out of its original alignment. However, for small projects which can be worked wholly within the circle of the top hoop, they can be useful. This type of frame is small, light in weight, and easily portable. There are many which are attached to a sewing bird. The sewing bird clamps onto the edge of a table top and holds the hoop. Both hands are left free to work on the canvas. A rotating frame is most commonly used with needlepoint. The top of the canvas is attached to the scroll rod at the top, and the bottom of the canvas is attached to the scroll rod at the bottom nearest the needlepointer. The rods can be rolled, so that the canvas is rolled around them. Only the area to be worked on is left exposed in the center of the frame between the two scroll rods. The rods are usually secured with screw nuts, clamps, or other similar devices. As a portion of the canvas is completed, it is simply rolled around one of the scroll rods and the adjacent unfinished portion of the canvas is exposed in the center to be worked on. The rotating frames are available in a variety of lengths. They are also light in weight and easily portable. It may take some practice to find a comfortable position to hold them in, since they are not attached to any permanent holding device. Usually one end is placed in the lap, and the other end is propped against a table or chair.

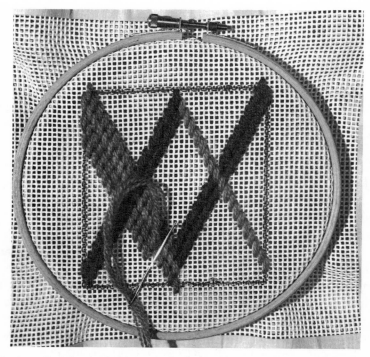

10. *A small design worked in a standard embroidery hoop. The size of the design should be limited to the interior diameter of the hoop. Because thicknesses of canvas vary, a hoop with adjustment screws is advisable.*

ARTIST STRETCHERS

One of the most inexpensive, and readily available frames that can be used are Artist Stretchers. They are frames used by artists to stretch their canvas before painting. They are available in art stores, or the art department of major department stores. They consist of separate pieces of slotted wood, available in lengths of from several inches to several feet in length. They can be purchased in pairs of varying lengths, and combined at will depending on the size of the canvas. The canvas may be tacked or stapled to the frames. When the canvas is completed, the frames may be disassembled and stored in a minimum of space. Similar to the rotating frame, the frame should be propped in the lap and leaned against some support.

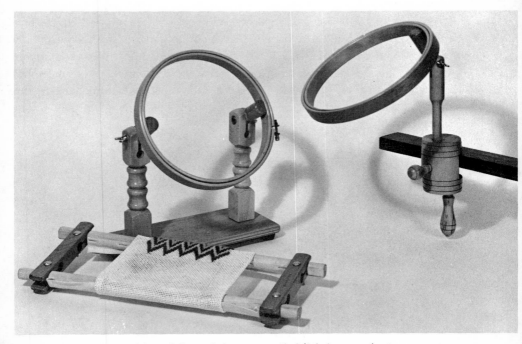

11. Small rolling frame with partially worked canvas attached (left foreground). As the design is worked, it is rolled onto the back roller and fresh canvas is unrolled from the front roller. The two embroidery hoops in the rear are either freestanding to use on top of table, or may be attached to the table edge..

RUG FRAMES

Perhaps the most convenient of all frames is the floor-standing rug frame. Almost all but the smallest of projects can be worked equally well on the floor frame. Similar to the rotating frame, the canvas is attached to the front and back revolving rods. However, the revolving rods are mounted on a floor stand. The height, angle, and position of the arms can be varied, depending upon the person's own comfort. Both hands are left completely free for manipulating the needle and thread. Many rug frames come with their own light attachments. The revolving arms and their supports make admirable places upon which to hang the yarn as you work. These frames may also be disassembled for easy storage. For any serious needlepointer, the investment of a few dollars in a frame of some type will produce years of comfort and superior needlepoint. While it is often argued that when needlepoint is placed on a frame, two separate motions are required for every stitch, thereby greatly slowing down the process; this may be overcome by allowing a small amount of slack in the canvas on the frame. The needle can then be passed down through the canvas and back to the surface of the canvas with one distinct motion. The canvas will still retain its original shape.

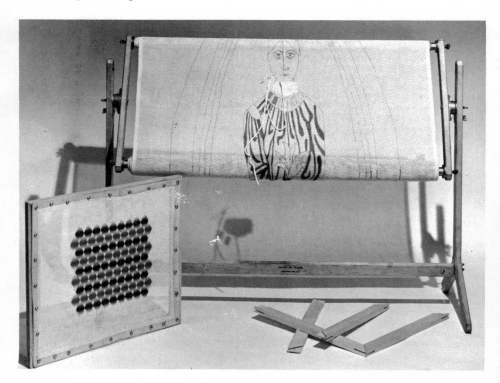

BLOCKING

While working on the canvas, it frequently becomes stretched out of its original shape. This may be due to the method of handling the canvas, or it may be that the stitches themselves have pulled the canvas crooked. Before the canvas can be finished and mounted, it should be stretched back into its original shape. This is called blocking. If the stitches have caused the canvas to become crooked, and if they have been pulled extremely tight, the process of returning the canvas to its original shape may be very difficult, if not impossible.

A flat, firm surface will be needed on which to tack or staple the canvas. The surface should be sufficiently large to give you ample working space on all outside edges of the canvas. An old drawing board, breadboard, or large piece of composition board are the most frequently used surfaces. The surface should be covered with paper. Secure the paper to the board with rustproof tacks or staples. These tacks or staples should be placed well outside the area to be covered by the canvas. It is essential that rustproof tacks or staples be used throughout the entire process. Otherwise, the water from the canvas will cause them to rust, and although they may be outside the canvas itself, the rusted water may run onto the canvas and permanently discolor it. Before the actual blocking is started, it is helpful to draw the outside dimensions of the canvas on the board. Then you will know how far the outside edges of the canvas will have to be stretched. Once this is accomplished, place the stretching board on a flat, stable surface. Place the canvas face down on the board. By placing the needlepoint face down on the board, the tension applied to the canvas during the blocking process will press the surface of the stitches flat. A much smoother surface of needlepoint will result. With a sponge or sprinkler, dampen the canvas thoroughly with cold water. Make sure that it is evenly wet. Do not apply so much water that it is saturated. Working quickly, tack one side down, matching the drawn outline of the canvas on the paper. Tacks or staples should be placed about 1 inch from the needlepoint area itself, and about 1 inch apart. If an adequate margin of canvas has not been left outside the needlepointed area, the blocking procedure will be extremely difficult. When one side has been tacked down, stretch the other corners as nearly as possible to the corners of the outlined area on the paper. Tack them down also. It may be impossible to pull the canvas entirely straight on the first blocking. Try to make it as straight as possible, however. Place tacks or staples, about 1 inch apart, around the remaining three sides of the canvas. Stretch all sides of the canvas as closely to the outlined area as possible. Once the canvas has been pulled and stapled or tacked down securely, place the board somewhere to dry. The board should remain horizontal, and in a cool dry place, exposed to the air, until dry. This may take several days. Do not be tempted to rush the process by placing the canvas in a very warm place. It will only cause the yarn to shrink somewhat and expose some of the canvas between the individual stitches. It will also increase the tension of the stitches and may cause the canvas to go crooked when removed from the board. When it is dry, remove the tacks or staples individually. Do not pull the canvas from the board. If you were unable to return the canvas to its original shape during the first blocking, the process should be repeated until the canvas is in the desired shape. Once the blocking has been satisfactorily completed, the canvas should be made into its finished form as quickly as possible. If you intend to store the canvas for some time, do not fold it. The creases may be very difficult to remove later on. Instead, cover the canvas with tissue paper, and roll the canvas loosely upon itself. The finished side should be rolled on the inside. It may then be slipped into a plastic bag, and kept wrinkle-free, until you are ready to use it.

QUESTIONS

Before any one of the projects outlined in this book, or any other project, is begun, there are several questions which should be answered. These may help prevent the waste of a great deal of time and money through inadequate planning or lack of understanding of the nature of the materials or techniques involved.

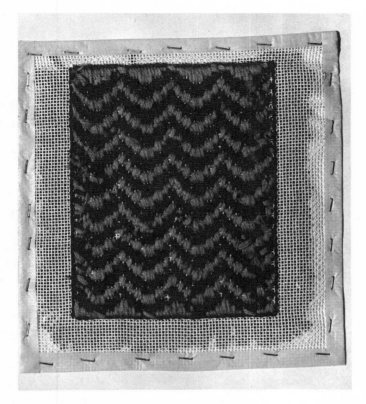

13. Needlepoint blocked, face down, as described. The edges of the canvas have been finished with masking tape to prevent unraveling. Staples hold the canvas straight.

1. How much wear and tear will the final project receive?

If the canvas is to be used on something which will be exposed to a great deal of stress and strain, then only the toughest yarns should be employed. A yarn which will produce a beautiful design, but does not stand up to constant use would be a poor investment. On the other hand, if the project is designed as a wall hanging, or other similar use where it will be exposed to a minimum of wear, then novelty yarns may be incorporated with little thought given to their strength. The length of stitches should also be considered. The longer the stitch, the more apt it is to catch onto something and be pulled out. Generally, the shorter, tighter stitches should be used for projects like book covers, book markers, bracelets, etc. On wall hangings or other similar projects, much longer stitches can and frequently should be. used. The strength of the canvas should also be considered. Only a tough durable canvas should be used for a rug. On smaller, finer projects, choose a fine mesh, thinner thread canvas.

2. How much money do I have to spend on a given project?

Since the canvas and yarns may run into a great sum of money on the larger projects, one should decide how much one wants to spend before selecting the type of yarn, or the size of the project. Only by working a small sample of the pattern on the size canvas that you anticipate using can you decide how much yarn you may need. This is one of the many advantages of having a sampler at hand at all times. Endeavor to estimate the entire cost of the project before beginning, including the cost of the yarn, canvas, mounting materials, and the blocking and mounting itself.

It is not advisable to purchase the yarn as you progress on a project for two distinct reasons. The first is that the dye lots do not always match. While some variation in color may be allowed in certain patterns, often the variations between dye lots may be so great as to suggest entirely different shades. Secondly, manufacturers are notorious for changing their production, introducing new yarns, dropping old yarns, changing color schemes, etc. If the yarn that you select for a given design is no longer available, you may have an extremely difficult, if not impossible job of finding matching yarn. Then you are faced with the prospect of abandoning the project in mid-stream, or somehow adapting the design to incorporate a new yarn or color scheme.

3. How much time will it take to complete the project?

Generally speaking, the smaller the stitch or canvas mesh, the longer it will take for the design to be completed. It naturally figures, that if a small stitch or mesh is used, it will take more time to cover a given area than if a larger stitch or larger mesh canvas is used. However, some patterns, due to their complexity, will take longer to work up than other patterns which may have smaller stitches. The designs which vary the stitch length, or which vary the length of the stitches in various bands, will take longer to complete than the designs which have a constant progression of stitches, or bands of stitches. Here again it is helpful to have a sampler and work several of the motifs before beginning the actual canvas to see if they are too time-consuming. A needlepoint project designed as a gift should give the maker pleasure. If a deadline is involved, and the stitches take much longer than anticipated, only frustration and a piece of badly made needlepoint will result.

4. Will the design be suitable for its intended use, or the recipient's taste?

Since one of the outstanding characteristics of Bargello is the repetition of various patterns, some thought should be given to the scale of the design, and its repetition. A pattern of stitches which covers many threads in each direction would not be very effective on a small project since there would be no opportunity to repeat and expand the pattern. Conversely, a small, highly-detailed pattern may be lost on a large project, such as a rug. Many of the designs incorporated in this book may be enlarged or reduced, depending upon the intended use, by choosing a different size canvas or by adjusting the length and placement of the stitches. Each change in canvas size or length of stitch will alter the final effect of the pattern. Here the sampler is useful.

Some consideration must be given to the use of color also. While traditional Bargello designs are known for the use of many shades of one color, or related colors, there is no reason why one cannot depart from this principle. If the canvas is designed for a modern setting, or for a person who loves bold, vibrant colors, the choice of soft, muted colors would be completely out of keeping. Many of the designs worked in this book have departed from the traditional shading of colors and would be appropriate in a more contemporary setting. In the reverse, many of the patterns would be just as lovely if worked in a softer, more harmonious combination of colors. It is best to work a small section of the pattern with the colors you anticipate using, to see the total effect of the size canvas, length of stitches and color relation.

5. *Will I be able to mount and finish the canvas when completed?*

One of the most expensive aspects of needlepoint is the blocking and mounting of the canvas when completed. Most of the projects in this book have been designed to eliminate this expense. Frequently the cost of mounting a project may far exceed the cost of the original materials involved. It must be remembered that if a person has enough dexterity to do the actual needlepoint, with some encouragement and instruction he or she will probably be able to block and mount the project. Of course, due to the nature of the material, there are some projects which require the hand and eye of the expert. Basically, needlepoint should be treated and handled as any heavy upholstery fabric would be handled. Needlepoint has the distinct advantage of being very, very strong. It will stand a great deal of abuse and still retain its good looks and wearability. If you have some doubt about your ability to mount the needlepoint when completed, inquire of a reputable craftsman concerning the cost. If the cost proves to be prohibitive, try a smaller version of the project and see if you can succeed in mounting it. If you resort to a professional, be sure that he is reputable and to be trusted with the needlepoint.

6. *Last, but certainly not least, can I do the design?*

Taking the ubiquitous sampler in hand again, sit down and try the pattern that you anticipate using. If it proves to be problematic, or you do not enjoy working it, try another design. If the design does give you a problem, and you are determined to use it, there are several ways to attack the problem. First, study the entire pattern to try to determine the relationship of each stitch to the preceding and subsequent stitch. See if they are the same length. Do they encroach upon one another by half their length? Is the encroachment consistant, or does it vary between the stitches. It may be helpful to draw the pattern out on graph paper to try to determine the relationship of the various stitches. Once this is accomplished, the pattern may be copied on the canvas. Each line on the graph would be considered a thread of the canvas. The pattern drawn on the graph can be copied, stitch by stitch on the canvas. If you still have trouble, consult an experienced needleworker, or possibly a shop specializing in art needlework. Many times these shops will offer free instructions to the novice.

III Stitches

Following are a selection of Bargello stitches and variations. Each has been presented with a sample of the stitch, and an accompanying diagram to show how the stitch is worked. While the variations on the stitches are probably endless, only a few of the more useful and simple ones are presented. Wherever the diagrams have numbers to indicate the sequence, the needle comes up through the canvas at the odd numbers. The needle then goes down through the canvas at the next consecutive even number. Some of the stitches are also supplied with letter designations. In these cases, the specific sequence will be outlined in the text accompanying the individual stitch. The Bargello stitches are differentiated from the needlepoint stitches in that they are worked parallel to the canvas threads, and usually are worked in a given sequence of colors and stitches. In the diagrams accompanying the stitch samples, the fine lines of the graph represent the threads of the canvas. The darker lines superimposed on the graph represent the actual stitch. By following the numbers or letters, the proper sequence of motions involved in the making of each stitch can be learned.

GOBELIN

One of the oldest stitches known, the Gobelin has many uses in Bargello needlepoint. The stitch consists of a row of straight stitches, all the same length, placed side by side on the canvas. Its main advantage is that it is very quick to do, and requires only a moderate amount of yarn. However, unless the yarn is suited just exactly to the canvas, the canvas will show through between the rows of stitches. The stitches should not be pulled too tightly. If yarn is used double, keep the two strands lying side by side. Do not allow them to become twisted on the face of the canvas. The stitches may cover any number of canvas threads. The needle comes up through the canvas at number 1. The needle is then passed down through the canvas at number 2. Follow the same sequence until all the stitches are completed. That is, bring the needle up through the canvas at the odd numbers and pass it back down through the canvas on the subsequent even numbers.

GOBELIN NO. 1
(Plate 14 and Fig. 7)

This sample stitch is worked over 6 threads of mono-canvas.

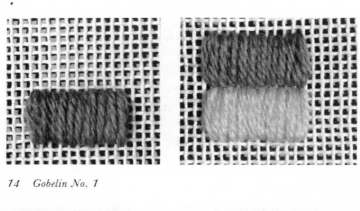

14   Gobelin No. 1

Fig. 7

Row 1

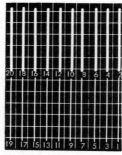

Row 2

GOBELIN NO. 2
(Plate 15 and Fig. 8)

This sample is worked on Penelope canvas. It will almost always be necessary to use many ply of yarn, or double strands of yarn, to cover the canvas adequately with this stitch. It should be used only where a much bolder effect is desired. With this stitch, the canvas is held in its customary position, that is, with the two warp threads running from the top to the bottom of the canvas.

15   Gobelin No. 2

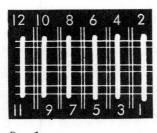

Row 1

Fig. 8

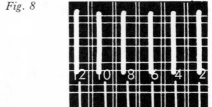

Row 2

GOBELIN NO. 3
(Plate 16 and Fig. 9)

This sample is also worked on Penelope canvas. The distinction between Gobelin 2 and 3 is that in 3 the canvas is turned on its side. The two warp threads run across the canvas. Stitches are placed between each of the woof threads of canvas. It results in a finer look than No. 2.

16   *Gobelin No. 3*

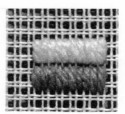

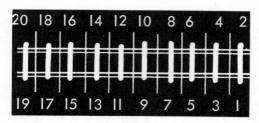

Row 1

Fig. 9

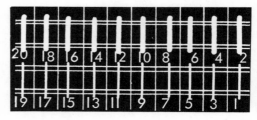

Row 2

BRICK

This stitch is similar to the Gobelin in that the stitches are worked vertically over the canvas threads. However, the rows interlock with one another. This eliminates the problem of the canvas showing through between the rows of stitches. It has a tendency to use a bit more yarn than the Gobelin No. 1. It is very quick to work, and wears well. The stitch may cover any number of canvas threads, but almost always covers an even number. The needle comes up through the canvas at No. 1. The needle is then passed down through the canvas at No. 2. Follow the same sequence until all the stitches are completed. That is, bring the needle up through the canvas at the odd numbers and pass it back down through the canvas on the subsequent even numbers.

BRICK NO. 1
(Plate 17 and Fig. 10)

This sample stitch is worked over 6 threads of mono-canvas.

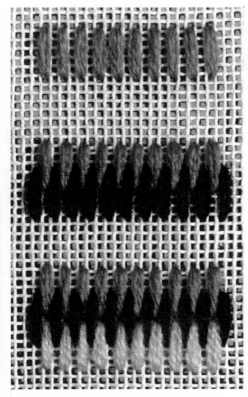

17 Brick No. 1

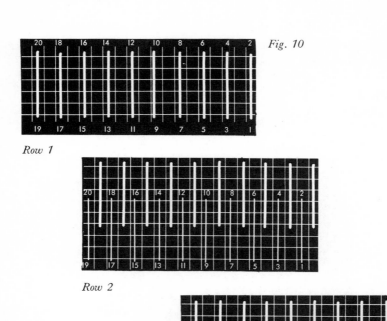

Fig. 10

Row 1

Row 2

Row 3

BRICK NO. 2
(Plate 18 and Fig. 11)

This sample is worked on Penelope canvas. It is particularly effective on large bold pillows or mug designs which require a big dramatic stitch. Either many ply of yarn, or double strands of yarn, must be used for this stitch. The canvas is placed in the traditional manner, that is, with the warp threads running vertical in the canvas.

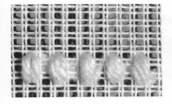 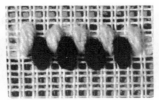 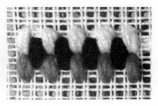

18   Brick No. 2

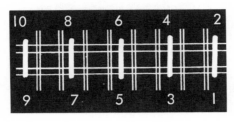

Fig. 11

Row 1

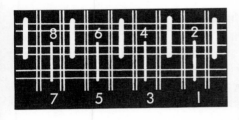

Row 2

Row 3

BRICK NO. 3
(Plate 19 and Fig. 12)

This sample stitch is worked on Penelope canvas. However, the canvas is turned sideways so that stitches are worked between each of the woof threads. The stitches cover the warp threads.

19   Brick No. 3

Fig. 12

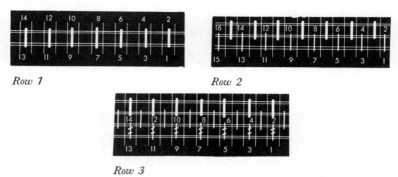

Row 1 *Row 2*

Row 3

FLORENTINE

This stitch is similar to the Gobelin except that the stitches are not worked side by side, but rather in diagonal bands which form peaks and valleys. When these peaks and valleys are worked in a graduation of shades and colors, the classic flame pattern is produced. The stitch is particularly quick and easy to do. It requires less yarn than the Gobelin or the Brick Stitches. They may cover any number of threads of canvas. The stitches usually cover an even number of threads. The stitches are then worked in a progression, either up or down, each stitch advancing by half the number of the stitch. That is, if the stitch covers four threads of canvas, the next stitch would be either up or down two threads of canvas. This is not a hard and fast rule however. The needle comes up through the canvas at number 1. The needle is then passed down through the canvas at number 2. Follow the same sequence until all the stitches are completed. That is, bring the needle up through the canvas at the odd numbers and pass it back down through the canvas on the subsequent even numbers.

FLORENTINE NO. 1
(Plate 20 and Fig. 13)

This sample stitch is worked over 4 threads of mono-canvas.

54

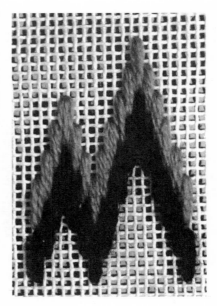

20 Florentine No. 1

Fig. 13

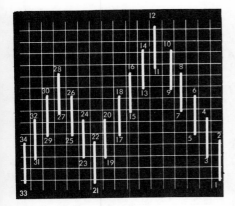

Row 1

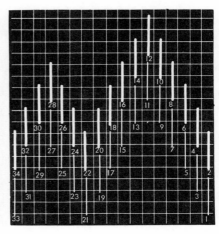

Row 2

FLORENTINE NO. 2

(Plate 21 and Fig. 14)

This sample stitch is worked on Penelope canvas, with the warp threads running vertically in the canvas.

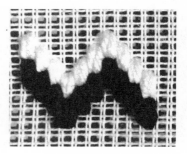

21 Florentine No. 2

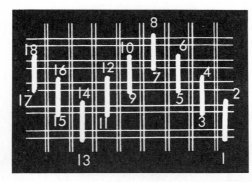

Fig. 14

Row 1

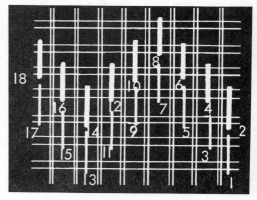

Row 2

FLORENTINE NO. 3

(Plate 22 and Fig. 15)

This sample stitch is worked on Penelope canvas, with the warp threads running across the canvas. Stitches are placed between each of the woof threads of canvas.

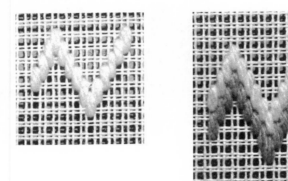

22   Florentine No. 3

Fig. 15

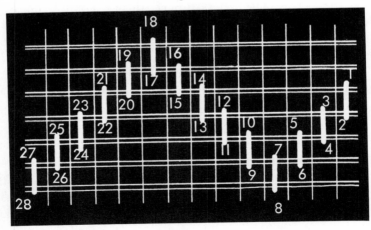

Row 1

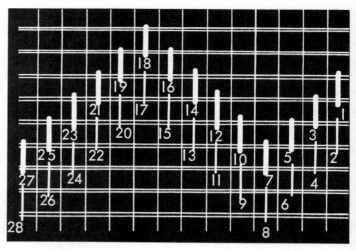

Fig. 15   Row 2

HUNGARIAN
(Plate 23 and Fig. 16)

This sample stitch is worked on mono-canvas. The stitches consist of one short stitch, followed by a longer stitch, followed by a final stitch the same length as the first stitch. A space in the canvas is left, and the same three stitch lengths are repeated. This sequence of stitches is continued across the canvas. The second row of stitches dovetails into the first row. The stitches in this sample cover 2 and 4 threads of canvas, but they may cover any given number of threads. The needle comes up through the canvas at number 1. The needle is then passed down through the canvas at number 2. Follow the same sequence until all the stitches are completed. That is, bring the needle up through the canvas at the odd numbers and pass it back down through the canvas on the subsequent even numbers.

The following stitches have been included to provide variety and additional textures when combined with the basic Bargello stitches. Many of them are slight variations of Bargello stitches. For example, the Encroaching Oblique is similar to the Florentine, except that the Encroaching Oblique slants across vertical canvas threads, whereas the Florentine is always worked between the two vertical canvas threads. This selection was in no way intended to be definitive. It is merely a selection of stitches which has proven to be practical, decorative, and easily combined with the Bargello stitches used through this book.

23 Hungarian

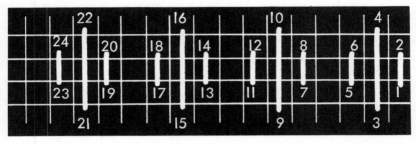

Row 1

Fig. 16

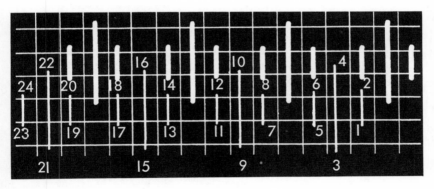

Row 2

CONTINENTAL

The Continental stitch is the most commonly known and used of all needlepoint stitches. It is quick to do, flexible in designs, and uses a moderate amount of yarn. The back side of the canvas is covered with a thick pad of yarn, which adds to its softness and wearability. The surface of the stitch is tight and will withstand a great deal of wear. Because the stitch is so short, it is difficult to snag. Its main drawback is that it tends to pull the canvas considerably out of shape. It can almost always be blocked back into proper shape, however. Work the stitch from the right side of the canvas to the left side. The canvas may then be turned upside down and the second row worked from right to left. The canvas is then returned to its original position, and the third row is worked again from right to left. This process is continued until the entire area is needle-pointed. The needle comes up through the canvas at number 1. The needle is then passed down through the canvas at number 2. Follow the same sequence until all the stitches are completed. That is, bring the needle up through the canvas at the odd numbers and pass it back down through the canvas on the subsequent even numbers.

CONTINENTAL NO. 1
(Plate 24 and Fig. 17)

This sample stitch is worked over the intersection of one warp and one woof thread of mono–canvas.

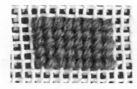

24   *Continental No. 1*

Row 1   *Fig. 17*

CONTINENTAL NO. 2   *Row 2*
(Plate 25 and Fig. 18)

This sample stitch is worked on Penelope canvas. The stitches cover the intersection of one pair of warp threads and one pair of woof threads. It makes little difference which way the canvas is held when this stitch is ‘used.

I.

II.

III.

IV.

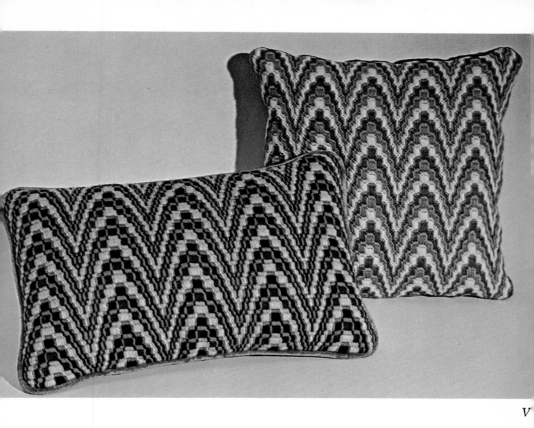

IX.

X.

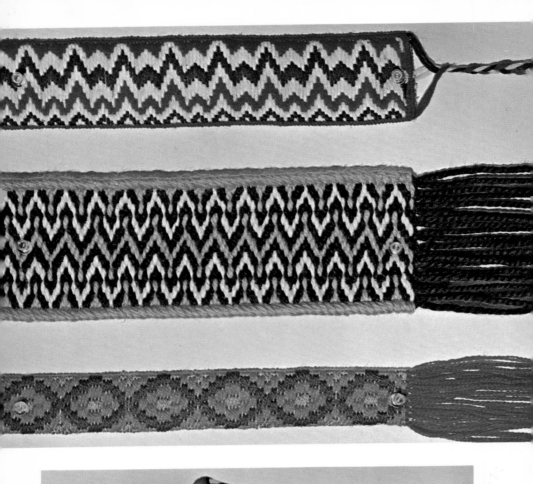

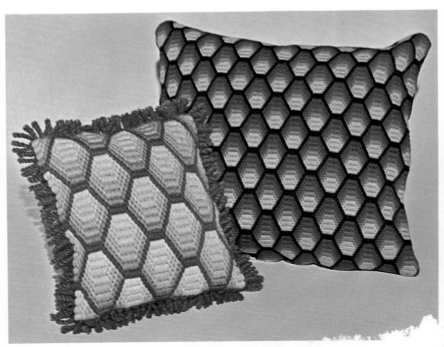

XV.

XVI.

25   Continental No. 2

Row 1

Fig. 18

Row 2

CONTINENTAL TRAMÉ
(Plate 26 and Fig. 19)

This stitch can be worked only on Penelope canvas. The yarn is brought up between two of the woof threads at *A* on the diagram. The yarn is carried across the face of the canvas for a short way and then is carried back down through the canvas between the same two woof threads at *B* on the diagram. This becomes the Tramé yarn. The Continental No. 2 is then worked over the intersection of the pair of warp and woof threads of canvas, and over the Tramé yarn. The needle comes up through the canvas at number 1. The needle is then passed over the Tramé yarn and down through the canvas at number 2. Follow the same sequence until all the stitches are completed. That is, bring the needle up through the canvas at the odd numbers and pass it back down through the canvas on the subsequent even numbers. The Tramé thread will give added depth and fullness to the stitch. The beginning and ending of the Tramé yarn should be staggered so that they do not produce ridges in the finished needlepoint.

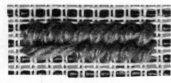

26   Continental Tramé

Fig.19

DIAMOND

This stitch consists of a series of stitches, beginning with a short stitch, followed with progressively larger stitches. When the longest stitch is determined, the length of the stitches is shortened progressively until you arrive at the length of the first stitch. Any number of stitches can be used. Once the length of the first stitch is determined, each progressively larger stitch will cover two more threads of canvas. Conversely, once the longest stitch has been determined, each progressively shorter stitch will cover two fewer threads of canvas. If the stitch is used as a border, only half of the diamond will be worked. In this case the stitches grow progressively larger by one thread instead of two. The needle comes up through the canvas at number 1. The needle is then passed down through the canvas at number 2. Follow the same sequence until all the stitches are completed. That is, bring the needle up through the canvas at the odd numbers and pass it back down through the canvas on the subsequent even numbers.

DIAMOND NO. 1
(Plate 27 and Fig. 20)

This sample stitch is worked over 2, 4, 6, 8, 6, 4, and 2 threads of mono canvas.

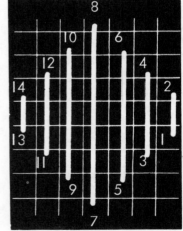

Fig. 20

27   Diamond No. 1

The half-diamond is used for a border. This sample stitch is worked over 2, 3, 4, 5, 6, 7, 6, 5, 4, 3 and 2 threads of mono-canvas to give one side of the diamond a straight line.

28 *Half Diamond*

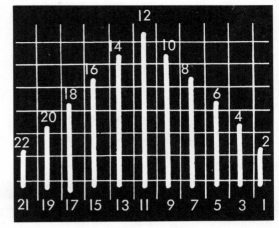

Fig. 21

DIAMOND NO. 2
(Plate 28 and Fig. 21)

Diamond No. 2 is worked on Penelope canvas over any number threads of canvas. The warp and woof threads may run either way.

WHIP

This stitch serves to finish off the edges of canvas when you do not want the canvas to be exposed when turning under. It also serves as an area, on the reverse side of the needlepoint, to which backing material may be sewn. The canvas is turned under, and the stitch covers the front, the edge and a portion of the back of the canvas in one stitch. The yarn is secured on the reverse side of the canvas, after blocking. The canvas is turned under. Bring the yarn out at *A*. The yarn goes through both layers of canvas at *B*. The yarn is then brought out at *C* and down through both layers of canvas at *D*. This process in continued until the end of the edge is reached. A second row of stitches, begun right beside the first, is worked in adjoining holes of the canvas. Finally a third row of stitches is worked in the remaining open holes of canvas. Each time the yarn is begun and ended on the back of the finished needlepoint.

WHIP NO. 1
(Plate 29 and Fig. 22)

This sample stitch is worked on mono-canvas.

29 Whip No. 1

Fig. 22

WHIP NO. 2
(Plate 30 and Fig. 23)

This sample stitch is worked on Penelope canvas. They may be worked across the warp or the woof threads, depending upon which edge is to be finished with this stitch.

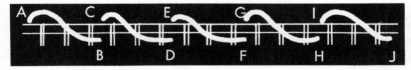

30   Whip No. 2

Fig. 23

TURKEY

Basically a rug stitch, the Turkey stitch has other uses. It is primarily used to finish off the sides or ends of projects since it produces a fringe effect. With some projects, such as belts and headbands, the ends of the Turkey stitch are left long and act as ties. With pillows and rugs, they merely serve as decorative fringes. If many rows of Turkey stitch are worked in a given area, the effect is that of a shag rug. This effect was used to simulate grass and trees in Hector the Lion. It creates an interesting contrast of textures when used with a flat surface stitch. The needle goes down through the canvas at *A*, up at *B*, down again at *C* and finally up at *D*. This sequence is repeated. Then the loops are cut and trimmed evenly.

TURKEY NO. 1
(Plate 31 and Fig. 24)

This sample stitch is worked on mono-canvas.

31   Turkey No. 1

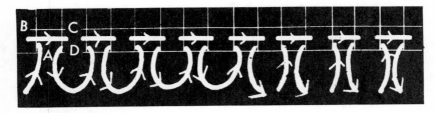

Fig. 24

TURKEY NO. 2
(Plate 32 and Fig. 25)

This sample stitch is worked on Penelope canvas. Each stitch picks up two threads of canvas. These may be either warp or woof threads.

32   Turkey No. 2

Fig. 25

SCOTCH
(Plate 33 and Fig. 26)

This is a quick, easy stitch to learn and do. Each stitch forms a small box when completed. They are effectively used in a checkerboard-type design. Unfortunately, it has a tendency to pull the canvas considerably out of shape. Because the center stitches are so long, it should not be used where there would be the possibility of it snagging easily. The sample is worked on Penelope canvas, but it is also effective on mono-canvas. The stitch uses quite a bit of yarn.

33
Scotch

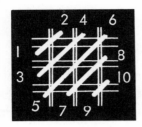
Fig. 26

REVERSED SCOTCH
(Plate 34 and Fig. 27)

This is just a reversal of the Scotch stitch. When the two stitches are used in conjunction with one another, an interesting contrast of textures is achieved. When used together, the problem of canvas distortion is also lessened.

In both the Scotch and Reversed Scotch figures the needle comes up through the canvas at number 1. The needle is then passed down through the canvas at number 2. Follow the same sequence until all the stitches are completed. That is, bring the needle up through the canvas at the odd numbers and pass it back down through the canvas on the subsequent even numbers.

34 · Reversed Scotch

Fig. 27

DOUBLE CROSS
(Plate 35 and Fig. 28)

This stitch consists of a large upright Cross-stitch, covered with a smaller diagonal Cross-stitch. It varies from the star stitch in that the diagonal Cross-stitch is smaller than the upright Cross-stitch. Because the large Cross-stitch is tied down with the smaller diagonal Cross-stitch, there is less problem with the stitch snagging. Unless the size of the yarn is closely matched to the canvas the stitch must be used in conjunction with other smaller stitches which cover the canvas. The stitch does not pull the canvas severely out of shape, and is not too extravagant in the amount of yarn it uses. It is particularly effective for accent. An interesting effect is achieved when the color of the upright Cross-stitch is different than the color of the diagonal Cross-stitch. The needle comes up through the canvas at number 1. The needle is then passed down through the canvas at number 2. Follow the same sequence until all the stitches are completed. That is, bring the needle up through the canvas at the odd numbers and pass it back down through the canvas on the subsequent even numbers.

35   Double Cross

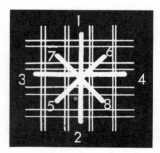

Fig. 28

KNOTTED STITCH
(Plate 36 and Fig. 29)

This stitch consists of one long diagonal stitch, tied down with a much shorter stitch, similar to the Continental stitch. While it may take considerable practice to learn the efficient use of this stitch, it is well worth the effort. The finished needlepoint has an extremely pleasing texture and durability. Because the long stitch is tied down with the shorter stitch, it is relatively free from the problem of snagging. The long stitches interlock with the preceding row of stitches on each subsequent row. The stitch is relatively economical in its use of wool. It does, however, have a tendency to pull the canvas considerably out of shape. The needle comes up through the canvas at number 1. It is then passed down through the canvas at number 2. Follow the same sequence until all the stitches are completed. That is, bring the needle up through the canvas at the odd numbers and pass it back down through the canvas on the subsequent even numbers.

36   Knotted

· Fig. 29

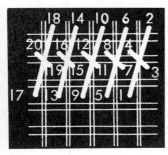

Row 1

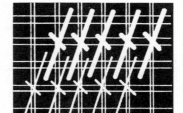

Row 2

WEB STITCH
(Plate 37 and Fig. 30)

The Web stitch is basically a Continental Tramé stitch worked diagonally on the canvas. The yarn is brought up through the canvas at *A* on the diagram. It is then carried diagonally across the surface of the canvas to *B* on the diagram. Then it is carried through the canvas to the back, and the Continental stitches are worked over the Tramé thread starting at 1 on the diagram. The needle comes up through the canvas at number 1. The needle is then passed down through the canvas at number 2. Follow the same sequence until all the stitches are completed. That is, bring the needle up through the canvas at the odd numbers and pass it back down through the canvas on the subsequent even numbers. The length of the Tramé thread should be varied so that there are no pronounced ridges on the surface of the finished needlepoint. The stitch is relatively economical in its use of yarn, and does not pull the canvas too far out of shape. The texture is similar to a woven stitch when completed. It results in a close, long-wearing piece of needlepoint.

37   Web

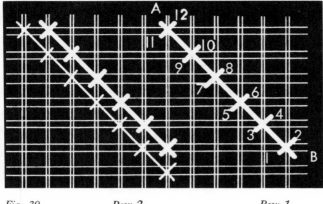

Fig. 30   *Row 2*   *Row 1*

SATIN

While this is basically an embroidery stitch, it is very useful for covering irregularly-shaped areas with solid masses of color and texture. It consists merely of a series of vertical or horizontal lines, of varying length, placed side by side. No particular thought is given to the length of each stitch. It merely covers a given area. The leading edges of the stitch may be treated in two manners; that is, they can be plain or they can be serrated. With a plain edge, the distinction between two areas of Satin stitch becomes pronounced and clear. Some of the stitches end in parallel holes. This may allow the canvas to show through if the yarn is not sufficiently full. With a serrated edge, none of the stitches end in parallel holes. They are purposely staggered so that the line between the two areas is less clear. The two areas interlock with one another. This is particularly effective where the shading of colors is supposed to be less noticeable. You will note that both types of Satin stitch have been used extensively in the Unicorn Tapestry. Where distinct lines in the foliage were desired, the plain-edge Satin stitch was used. Where the foliage was supposed to blend together, the serrated-edge Satin stitch was used. The needle comes up through the canvas at number 1. The needle is then passed down through the canvas at number 2. Follow the same sequence until all the stitches are completed. That is, bring the needle up through the canvas at the odd numbers and pass it back down through the canvas on the subsequent even numbers.

38   Satin No. 1 plain edge first and second rows

Fig. 31

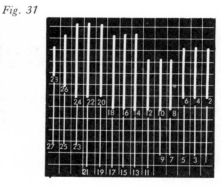

Row 1

Row 2

SATIN NO. 1
(Plate 38 and Fig. 31)
(Plate 39 and Fig. 32)

This sample stitch is worked on mono-canvas.

39   Satin No. 1 serrated edge first and second rows

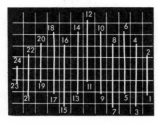

Row 1

Fig. 32

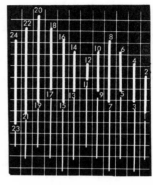

Row 2

SATIN NO. 2
(Plate 40 and Fig. 33)

This sample stitch is worked on Penelope canvas with the threads running in the conventional manner.

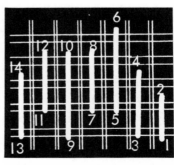

Fig. 33

STAR
(Plate 41 and Fig. 34)

This stitch should be used only for accent over a base of other, shorter stitches. Because of its long legs, it is very subject to snagging. If the legs are shortened, it can be applied to many more projects. This sample stitch is worked on mono-canvas, although it can also be used on Penelope canvas. The length of the legs can be varied at will. The needle comes up through the canvas at number 1. It is then passed down through the canvas at number 2. Follow the same sequence until all the stitches are completed. That is, bring the needle up through the canvas at the odd numbers and pass it back down through the canvas on subsequent even numbers.

41   Star

Fig. 34

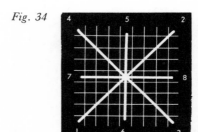

ENCROACHING OBLIQUE AND
REVERSED ENCROACHING OBLIQUE
(Plates 42, 43 and Figs. 35, 36)

This sample is worked on Penelope canvas, although the stitch may also be worked effectively on mono-canvas. It presents a pleasing, smooth texture. It is particularly effective where a pronounced direction of stitches is desired. With the Tiger Skin Cushions the two stitches were worked together to give the effect of the animal skin. Most of the yarn is on the surface of the canvas, and there is little backing. The stitch has a tendency to pull the canvas out of shape quite badly. However, the canvas is usually easily blocked into its original shape again. The needle comes up through the canvas at number 1. The needle is then passed down through the canvas at number 2. Follow the same sequence until all the stitches are completed.

That is, bring the needle up through the canvas at the odd numbers and pass it back down through the canvas on the subsequent even numbers.

42   *Encroaching Oblique*

43   *Reversed Encroaching Oblique*

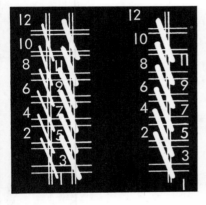

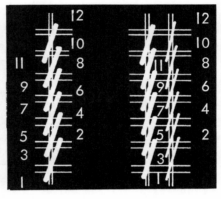

Row 2   Fig. 35   Row 1

Row 1   Fig. 36   Row 2

DIAGONAL KALEM AND REVERSED DIAGONAL KALEM
(Plate 44 and Fig. 37)

This sample is worked on Penelope canvas, but the stitch is also effective on mono-canvas. This stitch has little backing, and most of the yarn is on the surface. It presents a striking diagonal effect, and when the two stitches are used together, a handsome chevron pattern is formed. The stitch has a tendency to pull the canvas badly out of shape. The needle

75

comes up through the canvas at number 1. The needle is then passed down through the canvas at number 2. Follow the same sequence until all the stitches are completed. That is, bring the needle up through the canvas at the odd numbers and pass it back down through the canvas on the subsequent even numbers.

Row 1  Row 2

44   Diagonal Kalem and Reversed Diagonal Kalem

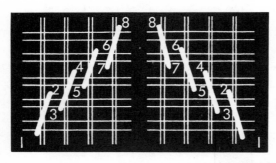

Fig. 37

Row 1   Row 1

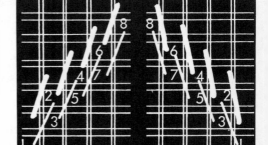

Row 2   Row 2

SLIP STITCH

After the needlepoint has been blocked, and the raw edges of canvas turned under to the reverse side, lining fabric may be attached to the reverse side of the needlepoint. Work the stitches close to the edge of the lining fabric. They should pick up a small piece of the edge of the finished needlepoint.

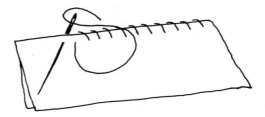

IV Home Decorating Accessories

WALL HANGING—THE UNICORN

Finished Size 36" by 52"

MATERIALS

> Knitting Yarn (Use the yarn double in the needle): Light Green—60 yards; Medium Green—30 yards; Dark Green—40 yards; Light Gray-Green—80 yards; Dark Gray-Green—30 yards; Red—10 yards; Blue—10 yards; Black—15 yards; Light Gold—12 yards; Dark Gold—10 yards; Charcoal—120 yards; Light Brown—30 yards; Medium Brown—20 yards; Dark Brown—240 yards; Light Olive—60 yards; Dark Olive—75 yards
>
> Cotton and Rayon Rug Yarn: White—250 yards
>
> 10 Mesh Mono-Canvas
>
> No. 18 Tapestry Needle
>
> Rug Needle
>
> Backing Material

STITCHES, COLORS AND METHOD

Follow Fig. 38, using this key. Tree No. 1: Light and Dark Green Kalem and Reversed Kalem. Tree No. 2: Light and Dark Gray-Green Encroaching Oblique. Work the background of the tree in dark gray-green and the spots in light gray-green. Neck Band is Red and Blue in Satin No. 1. Tongue is Red in Satin No. 1. Eye is Black in Satin No. 1. Horn is White Cotton and Rayon Rug Yarn in Satin No. 1. Hoofs are Light and Dark Gold in Satin No. 1.

(1) White Cotton and Rayon Rug Yarn in Satin No. 1. (2) Background: Dark Brown in Florentine No. 1 (each stitch is worked over ten threads of canvas). (3) White Cotton and Rayon Rug Yarn in Florentine No. 1, (each stitch is worked over ten threads of canvas). (4) Light Brown

in Florentine No. 1, (each stitch is worked over ten threads of canvas). (5) Light Brown in Satin No. 1. (6) Light Olive in Satin No. 1. (7) Dark Olive in Satin No. 1. (8) Medium Brown in Satin No. 1 (9) Medium Olive in Satin No. 1. (10) Light Green in Satin No. 1. (11) Medium Green in Satin No. 1. Top and Side Borders: Charcoal in Satin No. 1, (each stitch worked over ten threads of canvas). Bottom: Charcoal in Turkey No. 1. Instructions on finishing wall hangings follow.

45. Needleworkers have long been fascinated by the mythical unicorn—a horselike animal with a single amuletic horn in the middle of its forehead—and a famous series of tapestries woven in the Middle Ages dealt with its exploits. Our unicorn is worked in a variety of yarns with Bargello and other needlepoint stitches. Although the hanging is large, needlepointing time has been cut to a minimum by the use of extremely long stitches.

Fig. 38

The Unicorn

Tree No. 2   Tree No. 1

WALL HANGING—ETHEREA
Finished Size 27½" by 76"

MATERIALS

Knitting Yarn (Use double in needle): Light Gold—100 yards; Dark Gold—75 yards; Brown—200 yards; Black—100 yards; Gray —75 yards; Green—50 yards; Dark Blue—10 yards
Cotton and Rayon Rug Yarn: Cream—30 yards
Synthetic (Use the yarn double in the needle): Gold—30 yards; Red—10 yards
10 Mesh Mono-Canvas
No. 18 Tapestry Needle
Backing Material

STITCHES, COLORS AND METHOD

Gown: Work black areas in dark gold Florentine No. 1, each stitch covering eight threads of canvas. Work the balance of the gown in light gold, Florentine No. 1; each stitch covers four threads of canvas. Lily Head: Work with cream Cotton and Rayon Rug Yarns, using Satin No. 1. Lily: Stem: Work with green, using Florentine No. 1; each stitch covers eight threads of canvas. Lily Leaves: Work with green, using Satin No. 1. Hands: Work with the cream Cotton and Rayon Rug Yarn, using Satin No. 1. Shoulder clip, collar and crown: Work with the gold Synthetic, Satin No. 1, representing jewels. Neck: Work with cream Cotton and Rayon Rug Yarn using Florentine No 1; each stitch covers 8 threads of canvas. Facial features: Work in dark blue, using Florentine No. 1 over 4 threads of canvas, and Satin No. 1. Face: Work with cream Cotton and Rayon Rug Yarn, using Florentine No. 1; each stitch covers 4 threads of canvas. Hair: Work in black Satin No. 1.

(1) Brown Florentine No. 1; each stitch covers 8 threads of canvas.
(2) Black Florentine No. 1; each stitch covers 8 threads of canvas.
(3) Gray Florentine No. 1; each stitch covers 8 threads of canvas.
(4) Black Horizontal Satin No. 1. (5) Gray Horizontal Satin No. 1. Border: Work in black Satin No. 1. Instructions on finishing wall hangings follow.

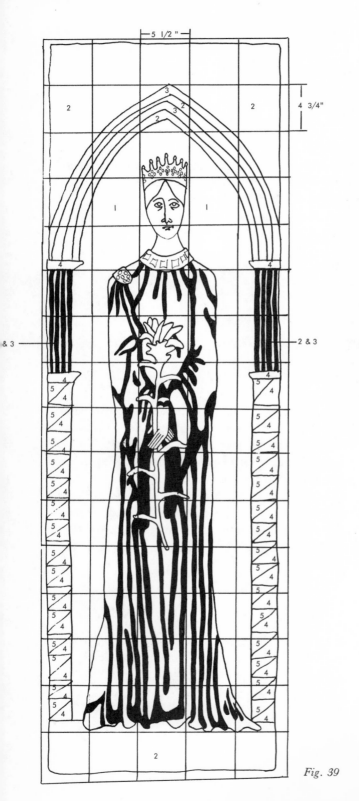

Fig. 39

WALL HANGING—THOMAS BEAUCHAMP
Finished Size 14" by 37"
(Not recommended for the Beginner)

MATERIALS

> Tapestry Yarns (Use yarn double in needle): Light Blue—120 yards; Dark Blue—75 yards; Red—50 yards; Light Turquoise—60 yards; Dark Turquoise—40 yards; Light Gold—60 yards; Dark Gold—60 yards; Black—200 yards
> 3-Ply Persian Yarn: Cream—25 yards; Black—5 yards
> Gold Synthetic Yarn (Use yarn double in needle): 40 yards
> 6-Ply Persian Yarn: Brown—10 yards
> Cotton and Rayon Rug Yarn: White—20 yards
> 10 Mesh Mono-Canvas
> No. 18 Tapestry Needle
> Backing Material

STITCHES, COLORS AND METHOD

Florentine No. 1 always covers six threads of canvas unless otherwise indicated. All colors are double Tapestry yarn, unless otherwise indicated.

Do eyes, eyebrows, and nose using Black 3-Ply Persian Yarn in Continental No. 1. Do background in Black Tapestry, Florentine No. 1. (1) Light Blue—Florentine No. 1 (2) Light Blue—Satin No.1. (3) Dark Blue —Florentine No. 1. (4) Dark Blue—Satin No. 1. (5) Red—Florentine No. 1. (6) Red—Satin No. 1 (7) Gold Synthetic—Satin No. 1. (8) Gold Synthetic—Encroaching Oblique and Reversed Encroaching Oblique. (9) Brown 6-Ply Persian Yarn—Satin No. 1. (10) Cream 3-Ply Persian Yarn —Continental No. 1. (11) Light Turquoise—Satin No. 1. (12) Dark Turquoise—Satin No. 1. (13) Light Turquoise—Diamond No. 1. (14) Gold Synthetic—Diamond No. 1. (15) White Cotton and Rayon Rug Yarn—Satin No. 1. (16) Alternate rows of White Cotton and Rayon Rug

Yarn, Light Turquoise and Red Tapestry Yarns—Florentine No. 1. The
White yarn covers two threads of canvas; the Turquoise and Red cover
four threads of canvas. (17) Dark Gold—Satin No. 1. (18) Light Gold—
Satin No. 1. (19) Dark Gold—Florentine No. 1, each stitch covering four
threads of canvas. (20) Light Gold—Florentine No. 1, each stitch covering four threads of canvas. (21) Alternate rows of Light and Dark Gold—
Florentine No. 1. Light Gold covers four threads of canvas; Dark Gold
covers three threads of canvas. (22) Black-Satin No. 1. Instructions on
finishing wall hangings follow.

*47 and Color Plate II. This tapestry of Thomas Beauchamp, Earl of Warwick, born
1345, was based on a memorial brass in St. Mary's Church, in Warwick, England.
A loyal servant of King Edward III, he plotted against the succeeding monarch and
was imprisoned in the Tower of London, in what is still known as Beauchamp Tower.
The tapestry has been worked in Florentine, Satin, Diamond and Continental stitches.*

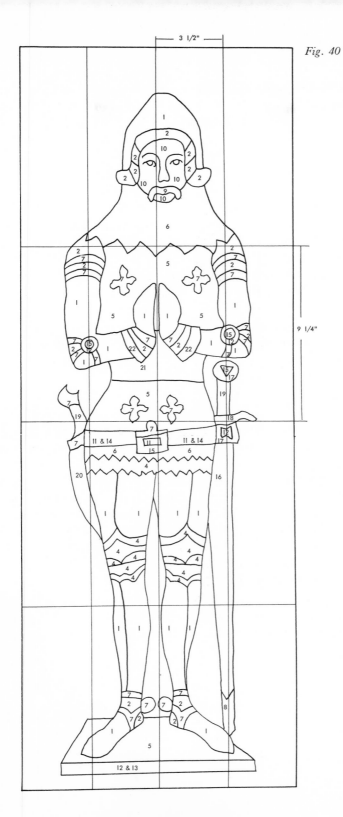

Fig. 40

WALL HANGING—MARGARET

Finished Size 14" by 37"
(Not Recommended for the Beginner)

MATERIALS

> Tapestry Yarns (Use yarn double in needle): Light Blue—25 yards;
> Dark Blue—5 yards; Red—60 yards; Light Turquoise—20 yards;
> Dark Turquoise—30 yards; Light Gold—25 yards; Rose—80
> yards; Black—200 yards
> Gold Synthetic Yarn (Use yarn double in needle): 40 yards
> Cotton and Rayon Rug Yarn: White—20 yards
> 3 Ply Persian Yarn: Cream—25 yards; Black—5 yards
> 10 Mesh Mono-Canvas
> No. 18 Tapestry Needle
> Backing Material

STITCHES, COLORS AND METHOD

Florentine No. 1, always covers six threads of canvas unless otherwise indicated. All colors are double tapestry yarn unless otherwise indicated.

Do eyes, eyebrows, nose and mouth with Black 3-ply Persian Yarn in Continental No 1. The background is Black Tapestry Florentine No. 1. (1) Light Blue in Florentine No. 1. (2) Dark Blue in Florentine No. 1. (3) Red in Florentine No. 1 (4) Gold Synthetic in Satin No. 1. (5) Cream 3-Ply Persian Yarn in Continental No. 1. (6) Dark Turquoise in Satin No. 1 (7) Light Turquoise in Diamond No. 1 (8) Light Gold in Satin No. 1. (9) Light Gold in Florentine No. 1 (10) Rose in Florentine No. 1. (11) Rose in Satin No. 1 (12) White Cotton and Rayon Rug Yarn in Florentine No. 1 (with each stitch covering four threads of canvas). (13) Dark Turquoise in Florentine No. 1. Instructions on finishing wall hangings follow.

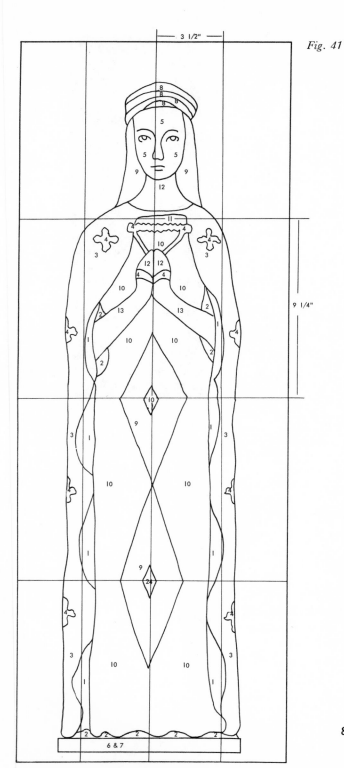

Fig. 41

3 1/2"

9 1/4"

87

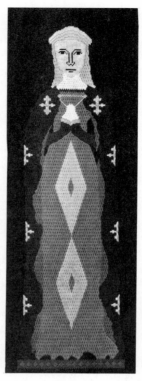

48 and Color Plate III. A companion to the wall hanging shown in Plate 47, this is of Margaret, Countess of Warwick, who died in 1406. It, too, is based on a memorial brass which is placed next to that of her husband. The tapestry has been worked in Florentine, Satin, Diamond and Continental stitches.

HERALDIC BANNER—CROSS DESIGN
Finished Size 13" by 17"

MATERIALS

> Paternayan Rug Yarns: Dark Blue—12 yards; Light Blue—20 yards; Red—40 yards
> 5 Mesh Penelope Canvas
> Rug Needle
> Backing Material

Florentine No. 3 is worked throughout over three pairs of warp threads. (1) Work Florentine No. 3 in dark blue. See Fig. 43 for top of cross and Fig. 44 for detail of cross arm. (2) Work Florentine No. 3 in light blue. (3) Plate 49 indicates six motifs at bottom of design. Work them in Florentine No. 3 in light blue. Invert Fig. 45 and place six motifs at top of design. Finish border with Satin No. 2, using light blue. Begin the cross at the top center, following the diagram. All the stitches in the cross and background follow the line of stitches established by the top of the cross. Instructions on finishing wall hangings follow.

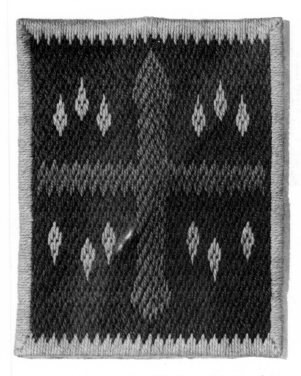

49. The simple forthright cross is enhanced by the rough texture of the rug yarn and the strict adherence to a basic Florentine stitch. The point at the top of the cross was established, and all the stitches follow its pattern. As in the diagonal band in plate 51, the Florentine stitches advance upon one another by less than half of the preceding stitch.

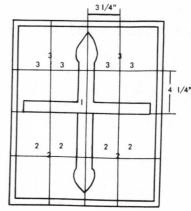

Fig. 42
Cross Design

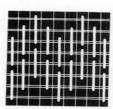

Fig. 43

Fig. 44

Fig. 45

Cross Design Motif

HERALDIC BANNER—FLEUR-DE-LIS
Finished Size 12" by 16"

MATERIALS

Paternayan Rug Yarn: Medium Purple—30 yards; Dark Purple—
20 yards; Blue—60 yards
5 Mesh Penelope Canvas
Rug Needle
Backing Material

Florentine No 3 is worked over 2 pairs of warp thread. The fleur-de-lis is medium purple in Florentine No. 3 The diagonal band is dark purple in Florentine No. 3. The background is blue, also Florentine No. 3. The border is medium purple in Satin No. 2. Instructions on finishing wall hangings follow.

50. *Complementing the delicacy of the fleur-de-lis, a shorter, tighter Florentine stitch is used. Each stitch advances by one-half of the preceding stitch. The slash of color across the face of the banner directly follows the line of Florentine stitches. You will note that a curved line can be only approximated when the Florentine stitch is used.*

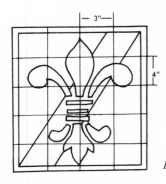

Fig. 46
Fleur De Lis

HERALDIC BANNER—DIAGONAL BAND
Finished Size 13" by 16"

MATERIALS

> Paternayan Rug Yarn: Light Purple—40 yards; Dark Purple—
> 30 yards; Yellow—15 yards; Light Blue—20 yards
> 5 Mesh Penelope Canvas
> Rug Needle
> Backing Material

STITCHES, COLORS AND METHOD

Florentine No. 3 is worked over 3 pairs of warp thread. See bands in
Fig. 47. Fig 48 indicates the placement of stitches. Each stitch advances
by one pair of warp threads of canvas. The line of the stitches will determine the diagonal bands across the face of the banner, and the placement of the other motifs. Put motif *B* on the dark purple band marked *B*
and work it in light purple. Put motif *D* on background marked *D*, in
yellow. Invert motif *D* on background marked *E* and work it yellow.
Finish the border in light blue Satin No. 2. Instructions on finishing wall
hangings follow.

*51. Diagonal Bands has been worked exclusively in Florentine stitch. The treatment
of the stitch is rather unusual in that each one advances up or down by less than half of
the preceding stitch. The stitch emphasizes and enhances the design and the color lines
follow the lines of the stitches.*

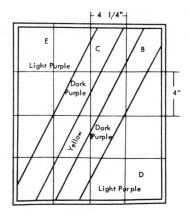

Fig. 47

Fig. 48

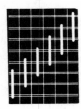

Fig. 49

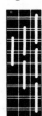

Motif B

Fig. 50

Motif D

WALL HANGING—AELFRED
Finished Size 14" by 16"

MATERIALS

> Tapestry Yarn: Black—30 yards; Cream—30 yards; Light Blue—
> 15 yards; Dark Blue—10 yards; Light Gold—12 yards; Dark
> Gold—10 yards
> Cotton and Rayon Rug Yarn: Cream—10 yards
> Synthetic Yarn: Gold—10 yards; Red—1 yard
> 10 Mesh Mono-Canvas
> No. 18 Tapestry Needle
> Wooden Dowels

The directions for Fig. 51 are as follows. (1) Use Black Tapestry Yarn in Satin No. 1. (2) Black Tapestry in Florentine No. 1; each stitch over 6 threads of canvas. (3) Cream Tapestry in Florentine No. 1, each stitch over 6 threads of canvas. (4) Light Blue Tapestry in Florentine No. 1, each stitch over 6 threads of canvas. (5) Dark Blue Tapestry in Florentine No. 1, each stitch over 6 threads of canvas. (6) Use Cream Cotton and Rayon Rug Yarn. Do fingers in Satin No. 1. Do hands in Florentine No. 1, each stitch over 2 threads of canvas. (7) Use Light and Dark Gold Tapestry. See Fig 52. Longer stitches represent the dark gold Florentine No. 1 over 3 threads of canvas. Shorter stitches represent the light gold Florentine No. 1 over 2 threads of canvas. These rows of long and short Florentine No. 1 are alternated throughout the cape. (8) Gold Synthetic Yarn in Satin No. 1 (9) Cream Cotton and Rayon Rug Yarn in Satin No. 1. (10) Cream Cotton and Rayon Rug Yarn in Florentine No. 1. Each stitch is over 2 threads of canvas. (11) Gold Tapestry in Satin No. 1.

Do eyes and nose with Black Tapestry in Florentine No. 1, each stitch over 2 threads of canvas. Do mouth with Red Synthetic Yarn in Satin No. 1.

After blocking, the edges of the canvas are turned under. Work the black Satin Stitch marked 1 in Fig. 53 over the edges of the canvas. Add a small black dowel at the top and bottom of the tapestry. Add four small tassels at each end of the dowel. Attach a string of black tapestry yarn to the top corners to hang the tapestry. Instructions on finishing wall hangings follow.

Fig. 51

Dark gold

Light gold

Fig. 52

Opposite 52. *This small wall hanging is based on one of the few existing monumental brasses of English royalty. Aelfred, who is depicted here, has been worked in a variety of Florentine stitches, each covering a different number of threads of canvas. Satin stitches have been used for accent.*

WALL HANGING—THE FANTASY GARDEN
Finished Size 16" by 40"

MATERIALS

> Paternayan Rug Yarn: Gray-Green—8 yards; Medium Red—10 yards; Dark Red—10 yards; Light Green—12 yards; Medium Green—16 yards; Dark Green—20 yards; Light Gold—7 yards; Dark Gold—7 yards; Light Blue—6 yards; Dark Blue—8 yards; Orange—10 yards; Pink—15 yards; Light Brown—40 yards; Medium Brown—35 yards; Dark Brown—35 yards
> 5 Mesh Penelope Canvas
> Rug Needle

STITCHES, COLORS AND METHOD

(1) Gray Green in single row of Encroaching Oblique and Reversed Encroaching Oblique. (2) Dark Red in uncut Turkey No. 2. (3) Dark Green in Encroaching Oblique and Reversed Encroaching Oblique. (4) Dark Gold in Satin No. 2. (5) Light Gold in Satin No. 2 (6) Light Green in Web. (7) Dark Blue in Scotch. (8) Dark Blue in Reversed Scotch. (9) Stitches 7 and 8 are outlined with a single row of Light Blue Continental Tramé. (10) Dark and Light Blue Double Cross. Each Double Cross has a stem of a single row of Light Green Brick No. 2. (11) Medium Green in Encroaching Oblique and Reversed Encroaching Oblique. (12) Dark Green in Encroaching Oblique and Reversed Encroaching Oblique. (13) Orange in Encroaching Oblique and Reversed Encroaching Oblique. All of No. 13 is outlined with a single row of Medium Red Encroaching Oblique and Reversed Encroaching Oblique. (15) Light Pink in Web. (16) Dark and Medium Red in Turkey No. 2. (17) Light Green in Encroaching Oblique and Reversed Encroaching Oblique. (18) Medium Green in Encroaching Oblique and Reversed Encroaching Oblique. (19) Alternating rows of Light and Dark Gold in Knotted. (20) Light Brown in Brick. Each stitch is over 2 pair of woof thread. (21) Dark Brown in Brick. Each stitch is over 2 pair of woof thread. (22) Medium Brown in Brick. Each stitch is over 2 pair of woof thread.

After blocking, turn under the two sides and top edges of the canvas and finished off with Medium Brown in Satin No. 2. Finish the bottom in Turkey No. 2, Medium Brown. Instructions on finishing wall hangings follow.

53. Fantasy Garden, worked with Paternayan rug yarns, was designed to incorporate a wide variety of stitches and resultant textures. In many instances, the shape of the stitch decides the shape of the design. Thus, the gold flowers are rectangular because the stitch naturally makes a rectangle. Conversely, the large tulip in the center assumes its own shape, and the stitches are worked out within it.

Fig. 53

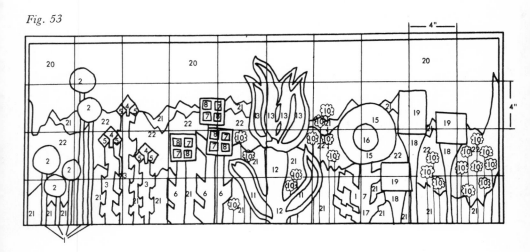

WALL HANGING—HECTOR THE LION
Finished Size 20″ by 36″

MATERIALS

> Paternayan Rug Yarn: Light Green—60 yards; Dark Green— 50
> yards; Light Gold—50 yards; Dark Gold—50 yards; Brown—30
> yards; White—1 yard
> Rug Needle
> 5 Mesh Penelope Canvas
> Backing Material

STITCHES, COLORS AND METHOD

Work Florentine No. 2 over two pairs of woof threads. The key to Fig. 54
follows. (1) Light and Dark Green in Turkey No. 2. (2) Light Gold in
Turkey No. 2. (3) Dark Gold in Turkey No. 2. (4) Light Gold in Florentine No. 2 (5) Dark Gold in Florentine No. 2. (6) Brown in Florentine
No. 2. (7) White in Satin No. 2. (8) Light Gold in Satin No. 2. (9)
Dark Gold in Satin No. 2. (10) Light Gold in Continental Tramé. (11)
Brown in Continental Tramé. Teeth: White in Continental Tramé. Background: Dark Green in Florentine No. 2. Instructions on finishing wall
hangings follow.

Opposite *54. Hector, the whimsical lion, designed for a summer cottage, has been worked ex-*
clusively in Paternayan rug yarns on rug canvas. It is an effective demonstration of the
textural contrasts possible through the skillful use of varied stitches. The lion's mane
and tail, and the grass and tree tops, have been worked with Turkey stitch. The lion's
body and the background of the forest were worked in Brick stitch. Where more detail
was needed, Continental Tramé and Satin stitches were used.

Fig. 54
Hector the Lion

INSTRUCTIONS ON FINISHING WALL HANGINGS

See the instructions on finishing rugs. Wall hangings may be finished in any of these three methods. In addition, they may be stretched on a backing board of some sort. The most commonly used is plywood. For smaller projects, use 1/4 inch plywood. For larger projects, use 1/2" plywood. After needlepointing and blocking the project, lay it face down on a secure working surface. Place the backing board on the back side of the finished needlepoint. Tack or staple the edges of the canvas to the reverse side of the backing board, checking to make sure that the backing board remains in the center of the needlepoint. Trim off the excess canvas on the reverse side of the backing board. The project may be framed, edged with upholstery trim, or hung as is.

For projects which are not hung on a backing board, a rod may be stitched across the back of the top of the hanging. This will act as a hanging device. Or a strip of velcro may be attached to the back of the top of the hanging. A similar strip of velcro may be attached to a piece of lumber the same width as the hanging. Attach the lumber to the wall, and press the two strips of velcro together. Drapery rings may be attached to the top of hangings as a decorative hanging method. The drapery rod may then be slipped through the rings and attached to supports on the wall.

PILLOW—GIANT SCALLOPS NO. 1
Finished Size 14" by 14"

MATERIALS

> 3-Ply Persian Yarn (30 yards of each color) : Gold, Dark Blue, Green, White, Yellow, Light Blue
> No. 20 or 22 Tapestry Needle
> 12 Mesh Mono-Canvas
> Backing Material
> Pillow Filler

STITCHES, COLORS AND METHOD

Step 1, Fig. 55. Using gold yarn, work the motif across the bottom of the canvas from one side to the other side. The stitches, Florentine No. 1 and

100

Gobelin No. 1, are worked over 2 and 6 threads of canvas. Step 2, Fig. 56. Using the dark blue, work the motif across the top of the base line established in Step 1. These stitches are also worked over 2 and 6 threads of canvas, but place them just opposite those established in Step 1. Following this color sequence: gold, dark blue, green, white, yellow and light blue. Repeat the sequence until you reach the top of the canvas area. Fill in the balance of the canvas with portions of bands, maintaining the same color and stitch sequence. Instructions on finishing pillows follow.

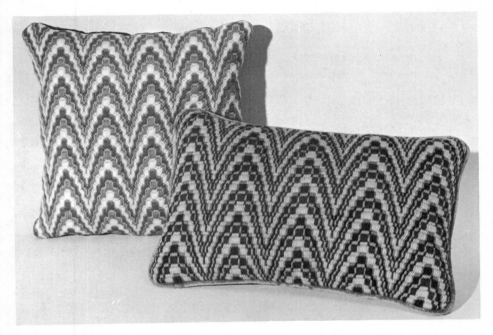

55 and Color Plate V. In the pillow in the rear, Giant Scallops I, courtesy Mrs. Bertram Glassner, stitches overlap stitches on both sides. Its variation (front) shows stitches placed diagonally on separate lines of canvas, above or below one another but not touching. Courtesy Mr. Arthur S. Lindo.

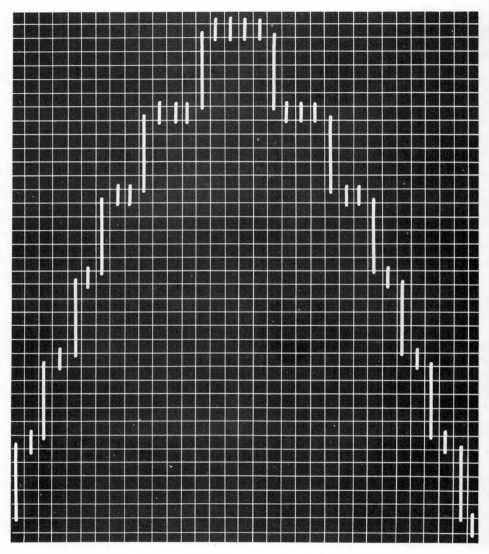

Fig. 55   Giant Scallops No. 1

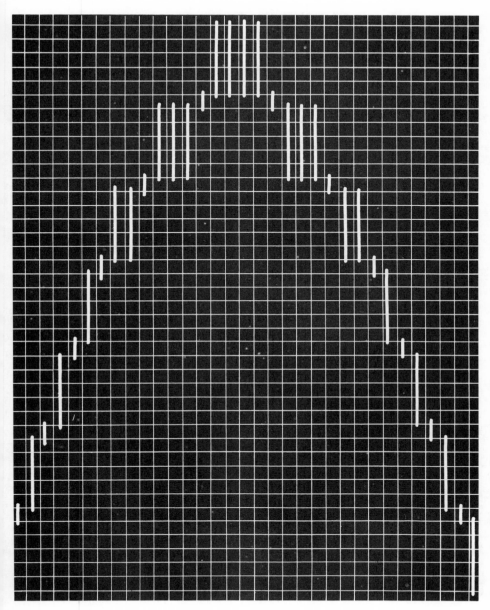

Fig. 56

Fig. 57   Giant Scallops No. 2

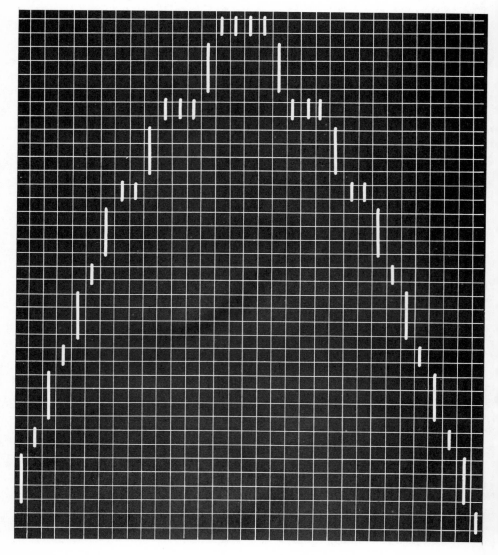

Fig. 58

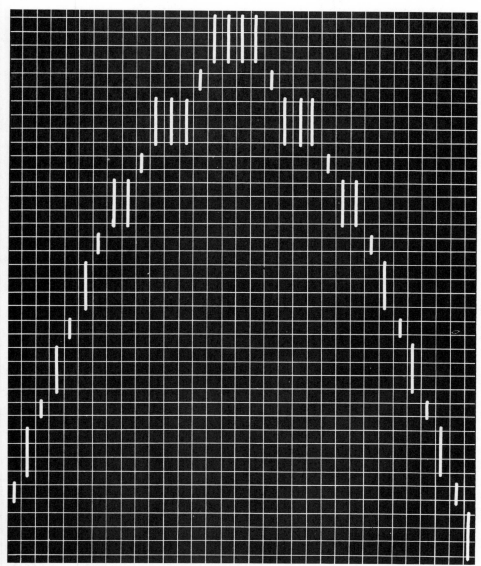

PILLOW—GIANT SCALLOPS NO. 2
Finished Size 12" by 16"

MATERIALS

> Tapestry Yarn: (20 yards of each color.) Orange, Brown, Yellow,
> White, Gold, Black
> No. 18 Tapestry Needle
> 10 Mesh Mono-Canvas
> Backing Material
> Pillow Filler

STITCHES, COLORS AND METHOD

Florentine No. 1.
Gobelin No. 1.
Step 1. Fig. 57. Establish a base row of these stitches across the base of
the canvas, using the orange yarn. You will note that this pattern of
stitches varies from No. 1 in that the stitches cover only two and four
threads of canvas, and that the stitches do not encroach upon each other.

Step 2. Fig. 58. Working with the brown, add this pattern of stitches
above the base line of stitches established in Step 1.

Continue, alternating Step 1 and Step 2 stitches, following this color
sequence: orange, brown, yellow, white, gold and black. Once all the
colors have been worked, repeat from the beginning again until the top
of the canvas is reached. The balance of the canvas is filled in with portions of bands, using the same color sequence.

PILLOW—VENETIAN BROCADE DESIGN
Finished Size 7" by 9"   *(Not Recommended for the Beginner)*
MATERIALS

> Knitting Yarn: White—16 yards; Yellow—8 yards; Orange—12
> yards; Black—40 yards
> No. 18 Tapestry Needle
> 10 Mesh Mono-Canvas
> Backing Material
> Pillow Filler

STITCHES, COLORS AND METHOD

Step 1. Work the heavy lines in Gobelin Stitch No. 1, using the white yarn. Careful counting is required since the stitches cover, 2, 4, 6, 8, 10 and 12 threads of canvas. Work one of the motifs in the upper left-hand corner. In order to determine the placement of additional motifs, it will be necessary to proceed through to Step 3. After completing the white portion of the motif, add the fine lines in the center of the motif. Work these in orange Gobelin Stitch No. 1. Careful counting is required since these stitches also cover 4, 6, and 8 threads of canvas.

Step 2. When the white and orange portions of the motif are completed, add yellow Gobelin Stitch No. 1, as indicated in Step 2. Place these stitches directly above the orange band completed in Step 1. These stitches cover 2, 4, 6, and 8 threads of canvas. Fill in the remainder of the center with black Gobelin Stitch No. 1.

Step 3. This small orange motif is placed between the larger white motifs. Begin the top of the motif, marked with a triple A in the spaces marked with a triple A on Step 1. Begin the bottom of the second motif, marked with triple B in the spaces marked with a triple B on Step 1. By counting the intersection of the threads between the respective motifs you will be able to determine the exact placement of the suceeding motifs.

56 and also jacket. Color can create three-dimensional effects. Bright warm colors advance toward the eye of the beholder; dark cool colors recede. In Shaded Crescents (left), the use of bright light hues at the outside top, shading to deeper tones, with a small cavelike area of black in the center creates strong perspective. In Medallion the flow of related color from light to dark, then light again, carries the eye gently in and out, thus creating an illusion of modified depth. Venetian Brocade has jagged forms and strongly contrasted colors which compel attention but create little third dimension.

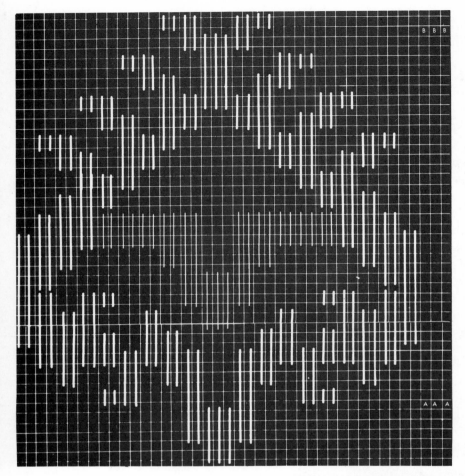

Fig. 59   Step 1

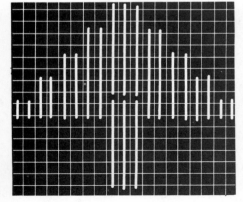

Fig. 60   Step 2

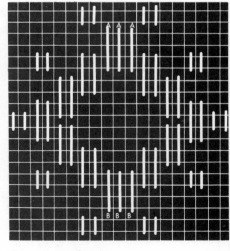

Fig. 61   Step 3

PILLOW—SHADED DIAMONDS
Finished Size 10″ by 10″

MATERIALS

>   3 Ply Persian Yarn (shades of one color, listed light to dark): 1.
>   Lightest—10 yards; 2. 15 yards; 3. 18 yards; 4. 22 yards; 5. 30
>   yards; 6. 35 yards; 7. 40 yards
>   No. 20 or 22 Tapestry Needle
>   12 Mesh Mono-Canvas
>   Backing Material
>   Pillow Filler
>   Upholstery Trim (Optional)

STITCHES, COLORS AND METHOD

Step 1. Use Brick No. 1 worked over 4 threads of canvas. It is essential
that the first row of stitches be placed correctly, since the entire diamond
pattern will be built upon them. Using the lightest shade in the group,
place one stitch along the top edge of the canvas. Each stitch should be
placed so that there would be room for 13 stitches to be worked between
them. That is, leave 13 holes in the canvas open between each of the first
row of stitches. These stitches are indicated by the heavy lines in Step 1
diagram. Directly adjacent, but lowered by two canvas threads, add two
more stitches in shade 2. They are indicated in the Step 1 diagram by use
of the thin lines adjacent to, and slightly lower than the heavy lines.

Step 2. Using shade 3, add three more stitches. These three stitches
will interlock with the second two stitches, and the center stitch will be
directly below the first stitch worked in Step 1. These stitches are indicated
by the heavy lines at the bottom of the Step 2 diagram.

Step 3. Using the shade 4, add four more stitches. These stitches will
interlock with the three preceding stitches. They are indicated by the thin
lines at the bottom of the Step 3 diagram.

Step 4. Using shade 5, add five more stitches. These stitches will interlock with the four preceding stitches. They are indicated by the heavy lines
at the bottom of the Step 4 diagram.

Step 5. Using shade 6, add six more stitches. These stitches will interlock with the five preceding stitches. They are indicated by the thin lines at the bottom of the Step 5 diagram.

Step 6. Using shade 7, add seven more stitches. These stitches will interlock with the six preceding stitches. They are indicated by the heavy lines at the bottom of the Step 6 diagram. This is the center, or broadest point of the diamonds. Reverse the procedure, working from the darkest shade to the lightest shade until the diamond pattern is completed.

Add the second row of diamonds, following the same procedure as outlined in Steps 1 to 6, beginning directly between the broadest portion of the preceding row of diamonds. The first stitch in the second row of diamonds begins at the "x" on the Step 6 diagram. Instructions on finishing pillows follow.

57. Shaded Diamonds has been worked for a pillow top, with colors shading from light points at each end to dark centers. This produces not only a diamond pattern, but also a series of bands across the center of each row of diamonds.

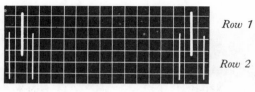

Row 1

Row 2

Fig. 62   *Step 1*

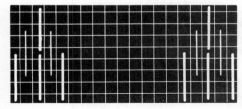

Row 3

Fig. 63   *Step 2*

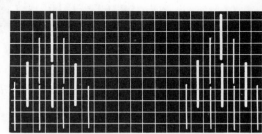

Row 4

Fig. 64   *Step 3*

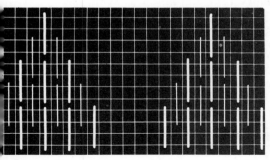

Row 5

ig. 65   *Step 4*

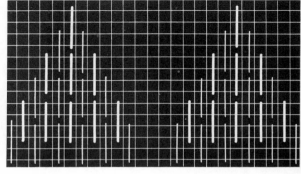

Row 6

Fig. 66   *Step 5*

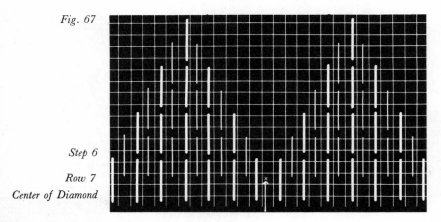

Fig. 67

Step 6

Row 7

Center of Diamond

Begin Row 2 of diamonds here

PILLOW—SHADED SQUARES DESIGN
Finished Size 13" by 13"

MATERIALS

    3 Ply Persian Yarn (5 shades of green listed light to dark): 1. Lightest—40 yards; 2. 30 yards; 3. 25 yards; 4. 18 yards; 5. 15 yards; Black—35 yards
No. 20 or 22 Tapestry Needle
12 Mesh Mono-Canvas
Backing Material
Pillow Filler

STITCHES, COLORS AND METHOD

Step 1. All stitches are worked over four threads of canvas. Diagram indicates the placement of the first band of Gobelin Stitches No. 1, worked in the lightest shade of green. Cover the entire canvas area with this pattern. All squares should be finished off at points at the top, bottom and sides to present a balanced pattern.

    Step 2. Work these stitches in shade 2; place them directly under the top of the squares which have been completed in Step 1.

    Step 3. Work these stitches in shade 3. Place them directly under the stitches completed in Step 2. You will note that the center of the square becomes smaller with the addition of each succeeding band of green.

Step 4. Work these in shade 4. Place them directly under the stitches completed in Step 3.

Step 5. Work these in shade 5. Place them directly under the band of stitches completed in Step 4. This should leave you with a small square at the base of the large square formed by Step 1.

Step 6. Work these in black. It completes the entire square. Instructions on finishing pillows follow.

58 and Color Plate XIII. Shaded Squares (rear) shows how a feeling of depth can be achieved by working a motif in several tones of one color, from the palest tint on the outside to the darkest tone at the center or bottom. (Courtesy Mrs. Bertram Glassner.) In Domed Spires, dramatic effect is created (with no attempt at three-dimensional quality) by strongly contrasted colors. (Courtesy Mrs. Jane Altman.)

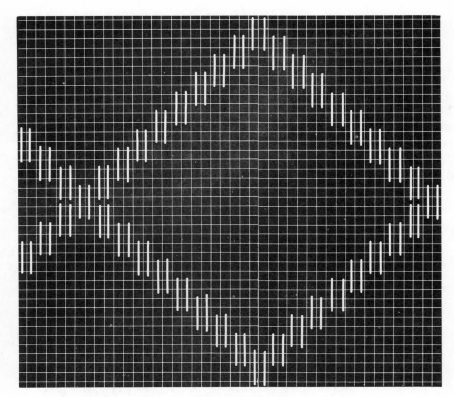

Fig. 68

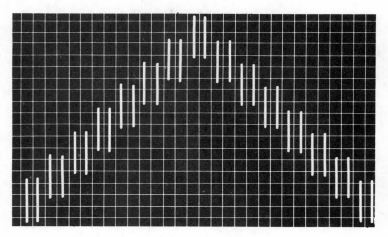

Fig. 69

114

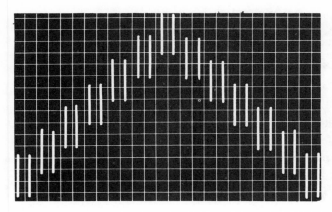

Fig. 70

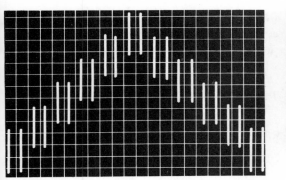

Fig. 71

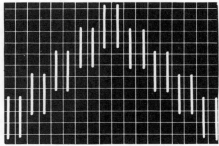

Fig. 72

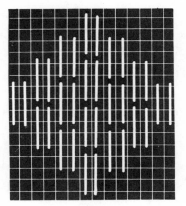

Fig. 73

PILLOW—DOMED SPIRES
Finished Size 12" by 12"

MATERIALS

> 3 Ply Persian Yarn: Purple—50 yards; Turquoise—35 yards; Olive—
> 30 yards
> No. 20 or 22 Tapestry Needle
> 12 Mesh Mono-Canvas
> Backing Material

STITCHES, COLORS AND METHOD

Florentine No. 1 and Gobelin No. 1 are worked over 4 threads of canvas.

Step 1. Fig. 74 indicates the placement of the purple stitches. The entire canvas should be covered with this open pattern. The individual motifs of the pattern should be completed at the top, bottom and sides of the canvas. This will result in a balanced design.

Step 2. Fig. 75. Add a band of turquoise stitches directly inside the motifs created in Step 1.

Step 3. Fig. 76. Add a band of olive within the turquoise worked in Step 2.

Step 4. Fig. 77. A second band of turquoise is worked inside the olive completed in Step 3.

Step 5. Fig. 78. The remaining 9 stitches are worked in purple and complete the center of each of the spires designs. Instructions on finishing pillows follow.

Fig. 74   Step 1

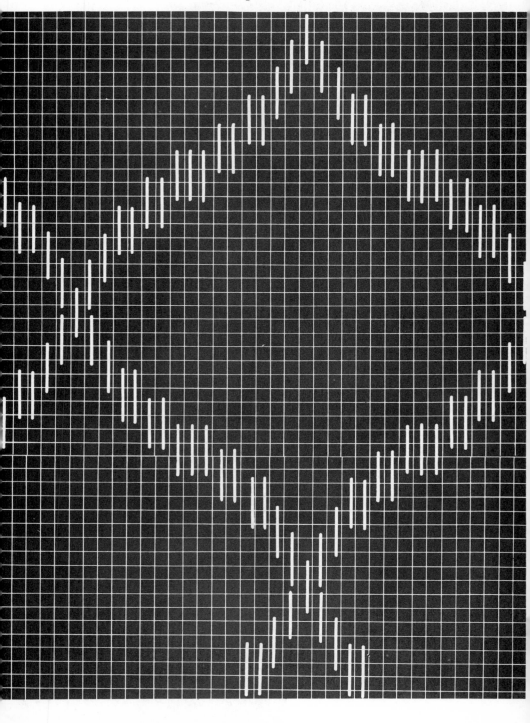

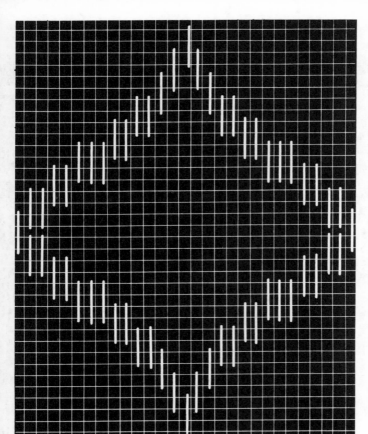

Fig. 75
Step 2

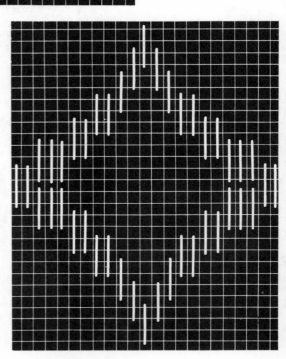

Fig. 76
Step 3

118

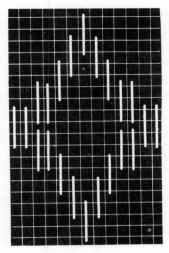

Fig. 77

Step 4

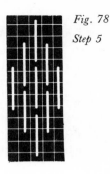

Fig. 78

Step 5

PILLOW—AUTUMN TREES
Finished Size 14" by 14"

MATERIALS

> 3 Ply Persian Yarn (4 Shades each of Green, Blue, and Yellow—All listed light to dark) : 1. Light—50 yards; 2. 35 yards; 3. 30 yards; 4. Dark—25 yards
> No. 24 Tapestry Needle
> 16 Mesh Mono-Canvas
> Backing Material
> Pillow Filler

STITCHES, COLORS AND METHOD

Use Gobelin No. 1

Step 1. Using the lightest shade of one of the colors, work this motif across the bottom of the canvas. Be particularly careful in the placement of the motifs since the second row of motifs will interlock with the first row. The stitches are worked over 2 and 4 threads of canvas.

Step 2. Using shade 2, work this scallop design directly on the top of the motifs created in Step 1. A second scallop, in shade 3 of the same color is added above the first scallop. Finally, a third scallop, using shade 4 of the same color is added above the second scallop. This will complete the entire first row of trees. These scallops are all worked over 4 threads of canvas. The bases of the second row of trees are placed directly between the tops of the first row of trees. They begin where the two *X*'s are placed on the Step 1 diagram. Continue the process of adding three darker scallops above these motifs. The third row of trees will be directly above the first row of trees. The color sequence of the rows of trees should be maintained once it is established. Instructions on finishing pillows follow.

59 and Color Plate XVI. Long Diamonds (pillow in back, described on p. 121), is one of the simplest and most widely used of Bargello patterns with the Florentine stitch naturally forming a diamond. The colors are shaded from light to dark, with an accent stitch in the center of each diamond. Courtesy Mrs. Rena Sherman. Autumn Trees represents a design of stitches adapted to conform to a pattern. In this case, the tree pattern was outlined and a sequence of stitches was placed within the design and repeated to form additional tree patterns. Courtesy Mr. Bertram Glassner.

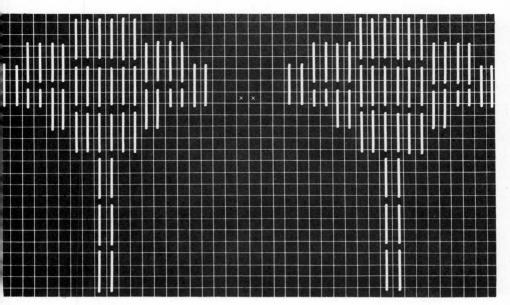

Fig. 79   Autumn Trees   Step 1

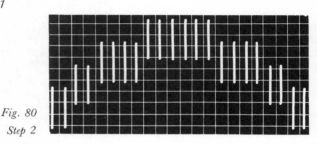

Fig. 80
Step 2

PILLOW—LONG DIAMOND DESIGN
Finished Size 12" by 12"

MATERIALS

    3 Ply Persian Yarn: Dark Green—40 yards; Medium Green—30
    yards; Light Green—25 yards; White—15 yards
    No. 20 or 22 Tapestry Needle
    12 Mesh Mono-Canvas
    Backing Material
    Pillow Filler
    Upholstery Trim (Optional)

STITCHES, COLORS AND METHOD
Florentine No. 1 is worked over 4 threads of canvas.

121

Step 1 indicates the placement of the dark green Florentine No. 1. The entire canvas should be covered with this open diamond pattern. Make sure that the top, bottom and side points of each diamond are completed. The pattern will be more attractive if each diamond is completed.

Step 2 indicates the placement of the second band of Florentine No. 1. This band is worked in medium green and is placed directly inside the open diamonds formed by Step 1.

Step 3 is a band of light green Florentine No. 1. This band is placed directly inside the open diamond formed by Step 2.

Step 4 is a band of white Florentine No. 1 placed directly inside the open diamond formed by Step 3. Finally, add one single stitch, covering 4 threads of canvas, directly in the center of this band of white. This should be medium or dark green.

Instructions on finishing pillows follow.

Fig. 81

Step 1

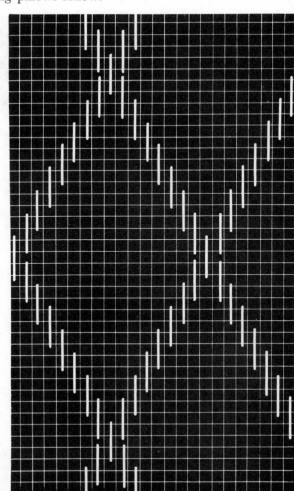

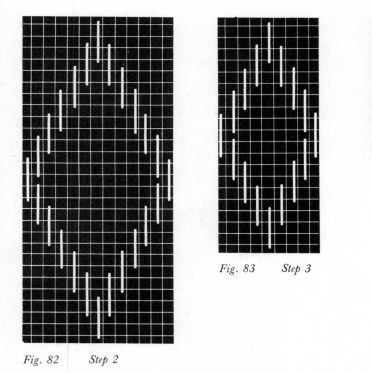

Fig. 84
Step 4

Fig. 83   Step 3

Fig. 82   Step 2

PILLOW—SUNBURST
Finished Size 15" in diameter

MATERIALS

Wool Tapestry Yarn: Red—50 yards; Orange—30 yards, Black—60
yards
Nylon Tapestry Yarn: Red—40 yards; Black—30 yards; White—6
yards
Synthetic: Blue—60 yards
12 Mesh Mono-Canvas
No. 22 Tapestry Needle
Backing Material
Pillow Filler

Use Brick No. 1 throughout. For black outline of face and black lines on face use Black Nylon Tapestry, with Brick No. 1 over 2 threads of canvas. (1) Blue Synthetic Yarn—Brick No. 1 over 4 threads. (2) **Red wool** Tapestry—Brick No. 1 over 4 threads. (3) Orange wool Tapestry—Brick No. 1 over 4 threads . (4) Black wool Tapestry—Brick No. 1 over 4 threads. (5) Red Nylon Tapestry—Brick No. 1 over 2 threads. (6) **White** Nylon Tapestry—Brick No. 1 over 2 threads. Instructions on finishing pillows follow.

60. An ancient Aztec design inspired this sunburst pillow. It has been worked in a combination of yarns—wool and nylon tapestry, and one of the popular synthetics. Brick stitches of varying lengths further enhance textural quality.

Fig. 85

PILLOW—NAVAJO DIAMONDS DESIGN
Finished Size 12" by 16"

MATERIALS

> Knitting Yarn (Use double in needle): Purple—30 yards; Red—
> 20 yards; Orange—20 yards; White—15 yards
> Rug Needle
> 5 Mesh Penelope Canvas
> Backing Material
> Pillow Filler

STITCHES, COLORS AND METHOD

Florentine No. 2 is worked over 2 pairs of woof threads. Starting at the
right side of the canvas, work one complete row of the diamond pattern
across the pillow, using purple Florentine No. 2. The diamond patterns
are actually made up of two distinct rows of stitches. Above and below
this row of diamonds, add one-half row of diamond patterns, using purple

Florentine No. 2. This will give you three rows of complete diamonds and two rows of half diamonds at the top and bottom of the pillow.

Fill in the center row of diamonds with the following bands of colors: 2 rows of red Florentine No. 2; 2 rows of orange Florentine No. 2, Center —white Florentine No. 2.

Fill in the next two outside rows of diamonds with the following bands of colors: 2 rows of white Florentine No. 2; 2 rows of orange Florentine No. 2; Center—red Florentine No. 2.

Fill in the two outside rows of half diamonds with the following bands of colors: 2 rows of orange Florentine No. 2; 2 rows of white Florentine No. 2; Center—red Florentine No. 2. Instructions on finishing pillows follow.

61 and Color Plate XIV. Bargello techniques lend themselves admirably to primitive designs. Two motifs from the American Indian, worked with large, bold stitches in Florentine and Gobelin, are shown. Navajo Diamonds (rear), was adapted from an ancient design and worked in brilliant contemporary colors for a New York apartment. Courtesy Mr. Arthur S. Lindo. Squares and Crosses (pillow in foreground; see page 108 for instructions), was adapted from a pre-Columbian design. It was interpreted in Paternayan rug yarns using lush greens and earth gold

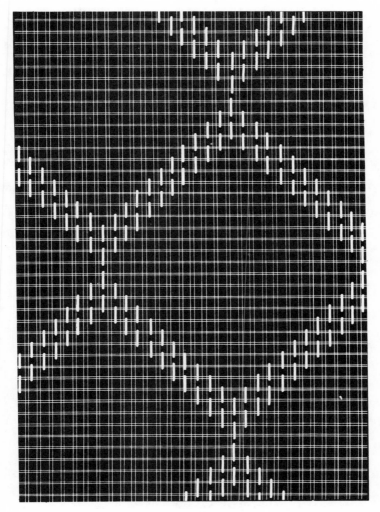

Fig. 86

PILLOW—TIGER SKINS
Finished Size 24" by 24"

MATERIALS

Paternayan Rug Yarn—Rust—40 yards; Black—40 yards; Gold—
60 yards
5 Mesh Penelope Canvas
Rug Needle
Backing Material
Pillow Filler

STITCHES, COLORS AND METHOD

Encroaching Oblique and Reversed Encroaching Oblique are worked in
the following colors 1. Rust, 2. Black, 3. Gold.

*62 and Color Plate VIII. Nature often inspires the designer. The cushions in the
wicker chair were adapted from a tiger skin with the direction of the stitches suggesting
the fur texture. The rug, Serrated Flame design (page 140), is one of many variations
on the basic flame pattern. Here the up-and-down lines of the flame have been inter-
rupted to form small plateaus halfway between the peaks and valleys.*

Fig. 87   Tiger Skins

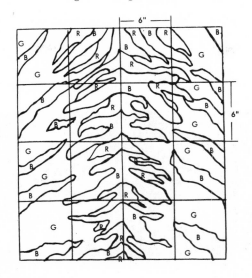

PILLOW—MEDALLION DESIGN
Finished Size 8½" by 13"
(Not Recommended for the Beginner)

MATERIALS

Paternayan Rug Yarn: Light Pink—12 yards; Rose—13 yards; Dark Lavender—14 yards; Medium Lavender—13 yards; Light Lavender—13 yards
Rug Needle
5 Mesh Penelope Canvas
Backing Material
Pillow Filler

STITCHES, COLORS AND METHOD

Florentine No. 3 is worked over 2 pairs of warp threads. The design indicates one complete motif, and the beginning of the adjacent motifs. Work 5 complete motifs in light pink across the face of the pillow. Add portions of the adjacent motifs above and below these five motifs. The balance of the design is completed by adding parallel bands of color inside and outside the light pink motifs. The color sequence inside the motifs is as follows: rose, dark lavender, medium lavender and light lavender. This will fill the motif to its center. The color sequence outside the motifs is as follows: light lavender, medium lavender, dark lavender, rose and finally pink. This will fill in the entire surface of the canvas. Instructions on finishing pillows follow.

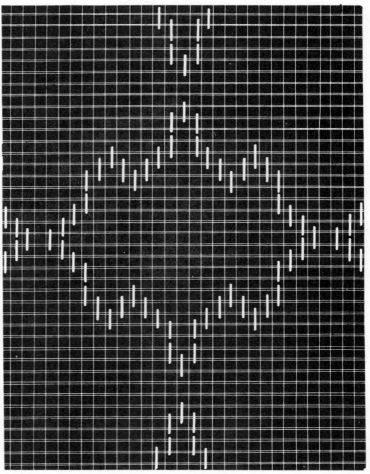

Fig. 88   Medallion

PILLOW—SQUARES AND CROSSES DESIGN

Finished Size 11" by 11"
(Not Recommended for the Beginner)

MATERIALS

Paternayan Rug Yarn: Light Green—18 yards; Dark Green—16
yards; Gold—30 yards; Brown Fringe—12 yards
Rug Needle
5 Mesh Penelope Canvas
Backing Material
Pillow Filler

STITCHES, COLORS AND METHOD

Gobelin No. 3 is worked over 2 pairs of warp thread. Step 1. The heavy
lines in the diagram indicate the placement of dark green Gobelin No. 3.
Step 2. The light lines in the diagram indicate the placement of light green
Gobelin No. 3. Step 3. The background is filled with gold Gobelin No. 3.
In order to cover the entire canvas with the design, it will be necessary to
find the repeat of the pattern and proceed from that point. Instructions on
finishing pillows follow.

Fig. 89   Squares and Crosses Design

*Opposite   63 and Color Plate XII. Shaded Hexagon interpreted with two widely divergent can-
vases and yarns. In the front, No. 1 is worked on rug canvas using Paternayan rug
yarns. Bold, contemporary and dramatic, the texture of the stitches is obvious even to
the casual observer. In the rear, No. 2 (courtesy Mrs. Bertram Glassner) is worked
on a small 14 mesh mono-canvas using Persian yarns. The effect is traditional, although
the color selection is contemporary.*

132

PILLOW—SHADED HEXAGON DESIGN NO. 1
Finished Size 9" by 10"

MATERIALS

> Paternayan Rug Yarn: Dark Gold—10 yards; Medium Gold—8 yards; Light Gold—16 yards; Dark Yellow—10 yards; Light Yellow —6 yards; Fringe—12 yards dark gold
>
> Rug Needle
> 5 Mesh Penelope Canvas
> Backing Material
> Pillow Filler

STITCHES, COLORS AND METHOD

Florentine No. 3 and Gobelin No. 3 are worked over two pairs of warp threads. Step 1, Fig. 90. Work it in dark gold, continue until the entire face of the canvas is covered with this open hexagon pattern. Step 2, Fig. 91, medium gold, is worked down the sides and across the bottom of each of the hexagon patterns formed by Step 1. Step 3, Fig. 92, worked in light gold, is added inside the band of medium gold formed by Step 2. You will note that there are two bands of light gold. Step 4, Fig. 93, is worked in dark yellow. It is added inside the band of light gold formed by Step 3. With this step there are also two bands of the color added. Step 5, Fig. 94, is worked in light yellow. It will fill in the balance of the hexagon pattern. This color also has two bands. Instructions on finishing pillows follow.

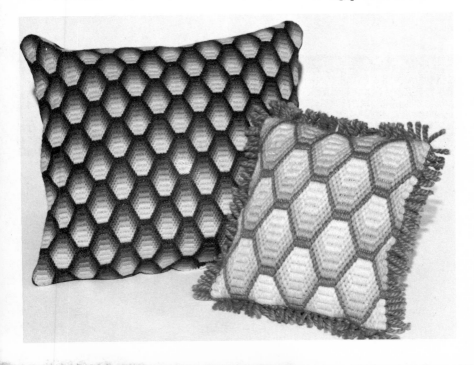

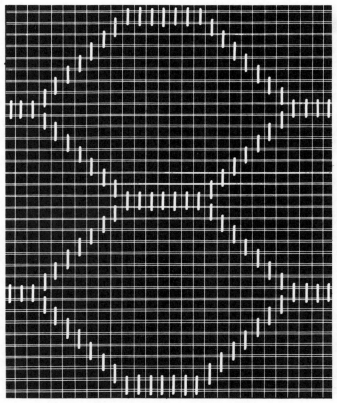

Fig. 90   Shaded Hexagon No. 1   Step 1

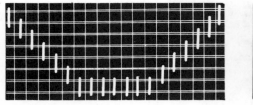

Fig. 91   Step 2

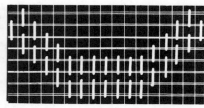

Fig. 92   Step 3

134

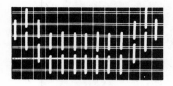

Fig. 93   Step 4

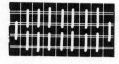

Fig. 94   Step 5

PILLOW—SHADED HEXAGON DESIGN NO. 2
Finished Size 15″ by 15″

MATERIALS

    3 Ply Persian Yarn: Charcoal Gray—25 yards; Dark Red—30 yards;
       Medium Red—25 yards; Light Red—20 yards; Medium Pink—20
       yards; Light Pink—40 yards
    No. 24 Tapestry Needle
    16 Mesh Mono-Canvas
    Pillow Filler
    Backing Material

STITCHES, COLORS AND METHOD

Florentine No. 1 and Gobelin No. 1 are worked over 4 threads. Step 1.
Following the diagram in Fig. 95, cover the entire face of the canvas with
charcoal gray. End the hexagons at the outside points and flat sides at the
top and bottom so that the entire design is centered on the canvas. Step 2,
Fig. 96. Work in the dark red directly inside each of the hexagon patterns
just formed. Step 3, Fig. 97. Work in medium red directly inside the
motif just completed. Step 4, Fig. 98. Work in light red directly inside the
motif just completed. Step 5, Fig. 99. Work in medium pink directly inside
the motif just completed. Step 6, Fig. 100. Work in light pink. These
stitches will fill in the bottom center of each of the hexagon patterns. Instructions on finishings pillows follow.

135

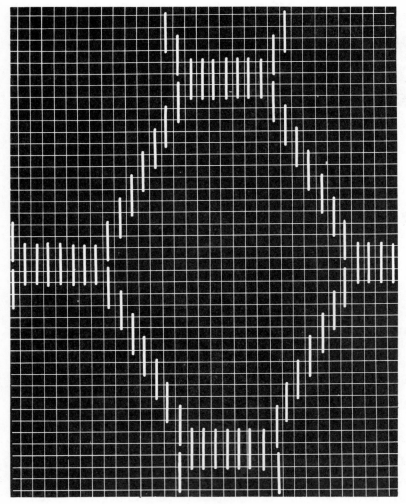

Fig. 95   Shaded Hexagon No. 2   Step 1

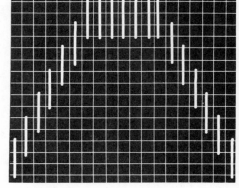

Fig. 96

136   Step 2

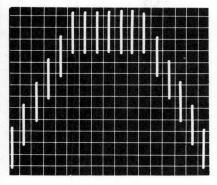

Fig. 97   Step 3

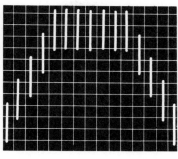

Fig. 98   Step 4

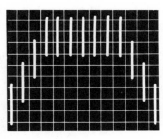

Fig. 99   Step 5

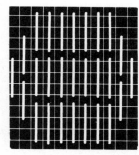

Fig. 100   Step 6

PILLOW—SHADED CRESCENTS
Finished Size 9½″ by 12½″

MATERIALS

>Paternayan Rug Yarn (Use double in needle). 5 shades of orange,
>listed light to dark: 1. Light Orange—12 yards; 2. 12 yards;
>3. 10 yards; 4. 8 yards; 5. Dark Orange—6 yards. Black—
>4 yards
>Rug Needle
>5 Mesh Penelope Canvas
>Backing Material
>Pillow Filler

Gobelin No. 2 and Florentine No. 2 are worked over 2 pairs of woof threads. Step 1, Fig. 101, indicates the placement of the lightest shade of orange. This pattern should be extended until the entire area of the canvas is covered. Step 2, Fig. 102, indicates placement, directly inside each of the crescents, of one band of orange. No. 2. You will note that the stitches in Steps 2-5 do not always cover the same number of threads of canvas. In Step 3, Fig. 103, you add one band of orange No. 3 inside each of the bands formed in the preceding step. In Step 4, Fig. 104, you add orange No. 4 directly inside the band formed in the preceding step. Step 5, Fig. 105 shows you where to add a small band of 5 stitches of the darkest orange (no. 5) inside the band formed in the preceding step. Step 6, Fig. 106, shows the final procedure—fill in the small eye with four stitches of black. Instructions on finishing pillows follow.

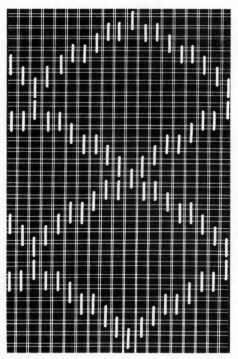

Fig. 101   Shaded Crescents   Step 1

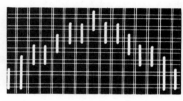

Fig. 102   Step 2

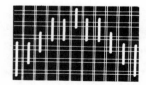

Fig. 103   Step 3

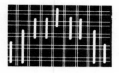

Fig. 104   Step 4

Fig. 105

Step 5

Fig. 106

Step 6

INSTRUCTIONS ON FINISHING PILLOWS

Needlepoint the design area. Block the needlepoint. If the pillow is finished with a Turkey stitch fringe, work the Turkey stitch now, being careful not to pull the canvas back out of shape again. Trim the raw canvas to within 1″ of the finished needlepoint. Be careful not to cut off the Turkey stitch. Turn under the raw canvas to the reverse side of the finished needlepoint. If felt is used for a backing material, cut the back the same size as the finished needlepoint, minus the Turkey stitch. Pin the backing material to the reverse side of the finished needlepoint. Slip stitch the backing material to the edge of the canvas. Leave a portion of one side open. Insert a pillow filler and slip stitch the opening closed. Because of the thickness of most needlepoint, it is difficult to use a sewing machine. If the edge is finished with Turkey stitch it will be impossible to use a machine. If a machine is available and can handle the thickness of the needlepoint and the backing material, place the blocked needlepoint on the backing material. The back side of the needlepoint and the back side of the backing material should be exposed. Pin the two together. Machine stitch around the needlepoint, keeping the needle just a fraction of an inch within the edge of the finished needlepoint. Leave a portion of one side open. Trim the canvas and backing material to within ¾″ of the machine stitching. Reverse the needlepoint and backing material, pulling both through the opening. Push out all corners and edges. Press. Insert pillow filler and slip stitch the opening closed.

The edges may be trimmed by stitching upholstery trim around the pillow. The yarn used in the pillow itself may be braided and used as a trim around the outside of the pillow. Tassels are often effective at the corners of the pillow.

RUG—SERRATED FLAME

Finished Size 16" by 42" plus fringe

MATERIALS

 Paternayan Rug Yarn (40 yards of each color for basic rug): Brown,
  Dark Gold, Medium Gold, Light Gold, Dark Yellow, Medium
  Yellow, Light Yellow
 Fringe: 90 yards Brown
 Rug Needle
 5 Mesh Penelope Canvas
 Backing Material

STITCHES, COLORS AND METHOD

Florentine No. 3 is worked over 2 pairs of warp thread: Starting at the
base of the canvas, work the motif across the entire width of the canvas
in brown. Work additional bands directly above this base line in the following color sequence: dark gold, medium gold, light gold, dark yellow,
medium yellow and light yellow. Then repeat color progression from the
brown. Fill in the open areas at the top and bottom of the canvas with
portions of bands, maintaining the same color sequence. After blocking,
the long edges of the rug should be turned under and slip stitched to the
back of the needlepoint. The ends are finished with brown Turkey No. 2.
The ends of canvas under Turkey No. 2 should be turned under and slip
stitched to the back of the canvas. Sew lining material to the reverse side
of the needlepoint. Instructions on finishing rugs follow.

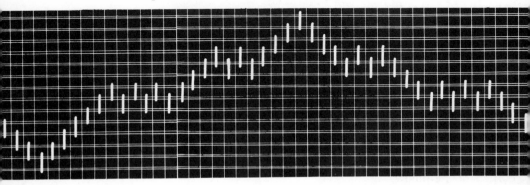

Fig. 107

INSTRUCTIONS ON FINISHING RUGS

Needlepoint the design area. Blocking the project may be a problem because of its size. Therefore, if at all possible, use a frame so that this step is not necessary.

To finish with a fringe, work the Turkey Stitch around the rug or on the desired ends. The fringe should be in proportion to the rug area itself. Turn the rug over, and trim the canvas to within 1″ of the finished needlepoint. Turn the raw edge under, and slip stitch to the reverse side of the needlepoint. If a lining is added, slip stitch to the edge of the canvas where it is turned under, covering all exposed canvas and yarn ends.

To finish with a Whip Stitch, turn the canvas under, leaving several threads of the canvas exposed. Work the Whip stitch through both layers of canvas. The corners will have to be covered with small triangles of Satin stitch. A lining may be attached to the back side of the rug. The edge of the lining material should be on the back side of the Whip stitch. In this way no canvas or yarn ends will be left exposed.

To finish with a plain edge, merely turn under the canvas. Trim to within 1″ of the finished needlepoint. Slip stitch the canvas to the reverse side of the needlepoint. The lining fabric will have to come out to the very edge of the rug if it is to cover all the exposed canvas. Care must be taken when it is sewn on to the rug that the canvas, lining and stitches are not exposed.

FOOTSTOOL—CHAIN DESIGN

Finished Size 14" by 16"

MATERIALS

> 4-Ply Persian Yarn: Dark Pink—50 yards; Medium Pink—35 yards;
> Light Pink—35 yards; Light Purple—25 yards; Dark Purple—
> 20 yards
> No. 18 Tapestry Needle
> 10 Mesh Mono-Canvas
> Footstool

STITCHES, COLORS AND METHOD

Florentine No. 1 and Gobelin No. 1 are worked over 4 threads of canvas. Step 1. This indicates the placement of the chain design across the canvas. It is worked in dark pink. The entire canvas should be covered with this design. Step 2. The heavy lines indicate the placement of the light pink stitches within the chain design formed by Step 1. The light lines indicate the placement of the medium pink stitches within the chain design formed in Step 1. The placement of the light and medium pink stitches alternates from one chain link to the next chain link. Step 3. The heavy lines are worked in dark purple between the chain design formed in Step 1. In the center of this open diamond pattern, work 4 stitches of light purple. After blocking, remove the top of the footstool. The top should be covered with suitable padding material. The canvas should be centered over the top of the stool. Tack the four sides of the canvas to the reverse side of the top. Check to see that the canvas is still centered. Tack the remainder of the canvas edges to the reverse side of the top. A staple gun will be helpful here. The canvas should be pulled tight so that there are no wrinkles on the sides of the canvas where it is wrapped around the corner. The top of the footstool is then returned to the footstool and secured in place.

64 and also jacket. Two distinct designs are used in one harmonious pattern on a foot-stool. Rather than surround the chain design (worked in shades of pink) with a dark quiet color, the background was done in vibrant purples. Thus background becomes as important as the main design.

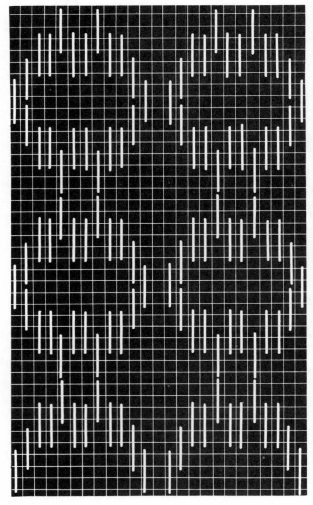

Fig. 108   Step 1

144

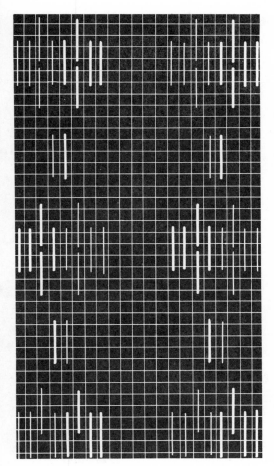

Fig. 109   Step 2

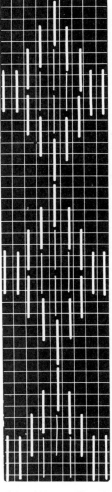

Fig. 110   Step 3

DESK SET—BROKEN FLAME DESIGN

MATERIALS

Large Fruit Juice Can 7″ high by 4″ Diameter
Medium Fruit Juice Can, 4¼″ high by 3″ Diameter
Small Fish Can, 1¾″ high by 3¼″ Diameter
3 Ply Persian Yarn: For Large Can—20 yards each of Red, Pink and
Orange; For Medium Can—10 yards each of Red, Pink and
Orange; For Small Can—5 yards each of Red, Pink and Orange
No. 20 or 22 Tapestry Needle
12 Mesh Mono-Canvas
Upholstery Trim
Glue
Paint

STITCHES, COLORS AND METHOD

Florentine No. 1 is worked over 4 threads. For the large can, needlepoint
an area 6½″ high by 13″ long. For the medium can, needlepoint an area
4″ high by 10¼″ long. For the small can, needlepoint an area 1¼″ high
by 10¾″ long.

Beginning at the bottom of the area to be needlepointed, work one
band of orange Florentine No. 1 across the entire length of the canvas.
Add a second band above this of pink Florentine No. 1. The third band
will be red Florentine No. 1. Continue this color progression until the
top of the canvas area to be needlepointed is reached. The open portions
of canvas at the top and bottom are filled in with portions of bands, always
following the same sequence of colors.

Remove the tops from the cans and clean throughly. Paint the inside
and outside with red paint, or other suitable color.

After blocking, turn under the top and bottom edges of the raw canvas,
and glue securely to the reverse side of the needlepoint. Do not apply an
excess of glue or it may stain the surface of the needlepoint. Trim off the
excess canvas to within ½″. Repeat the same process with the ends of the
needlepoint. Glue a band of moss fringe around the top and bottom of
each can. When all glue is thoroughly dry, wrap the needlepoint around

146

the cans and carefully slip stitch the two ends together in the back of each can. The stitching may be covered with upholstery trim if necessary.

65 and Color Plate VII. *The simple Broken Flame has been interpreted in brightest shades of red, orange and pink. The results, easily mounted on empty tin cans, become an attractive desk set. The design could be used for book covers, desk blotters, letter openers and other desk accessories.*

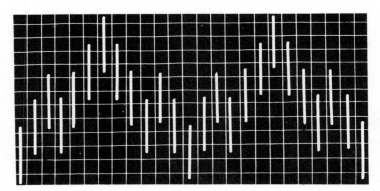

Fig. 111   Broken Flame Design

SMALL WOODEN BOX—PINE TREE DESIGN
Finished Size 3¾" by 4¼"

MATERIALS

> 4-Ply Persian Yarn (4 shades of green, listed light to dark): 1. Lightest—1 yard; 2. 1 yard; 3. 1 yard; 4. Darkest—2 yards
> Brown—1 yard
> Cream—22 yards
> No. 20 or 22 Tapestry Needle
> 12 Mesh Mono-Canvas
> Padding Material
> Upholstery Trim
> Small Wooden Box

STITCHES, COLORS AND METHOD

Florentine No. 1 is worked over 2 threads. The tree trunk, indicated by the heavy lines in the diagram, is worked in brown. The individual branches, indicated by the fine lines are worked from darkest green (Row A) to lightest green (Row D). The rows of individual branches are broken by the dotted lines. The 8 motifs in Row A are the darkest green; the 6 motifs in Row B are the next shade lighter green; the next 4 motifs in Row C are the next lighter green; and the top 2 motifs in Row D are the lightest green.

Instructions on finishing box tops follow.

66 and Color Plate X. To unclutter table, desk or bureau top, we show wooden boxes covered with Bargello patterns. The plain wooden boxes, available in most craft shops, are recessed to accommodate ceramic tiles, but we padded the top, tacked on the needle-point, and glued on some trim. The long box is a basic Lattice; the square box is covered with Pine Tree, an adaptation of an early American quilt pattern.

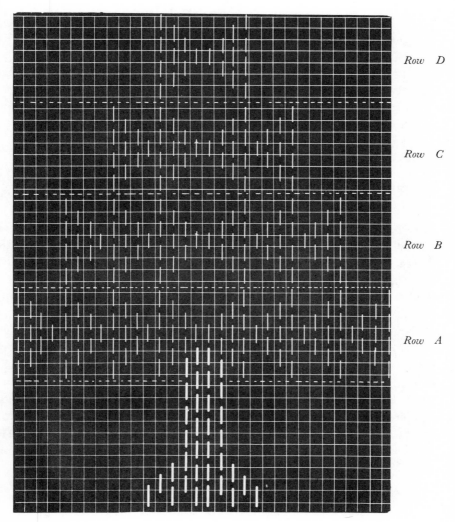

Row D

Row C

Row B

Row A

Fig. 112

BOX—LATTICE DESIGN
Finished Size 9" by 3½"

MATERIALS

3-Ply Persian Yarn: Black—6 yards; Brown—10 yards; Dark Gold—
9 yards; Medium Gold—8 yards; Light Gold—8 yards
No. 20 or 22 Tapestry Needle
12 Mesh Mono-Canvas
Wooden Box
Upholstery Trim
Small Tacks or Staples
Padding Material

STITCHES, COLORS AND METHOD

Gobelin No. 1 is worked over 4 threads. The thin lines on the diagram indicate the placement of brown Gobelin No. 1. To facilitate working this design, establish these bands of brown across the entire canvas first. Then add the cluster of 8 black Gobelin No. 1 as indicated on the diagram by the broad black lines. After the brown and black stitches have been completed, starting at the stitch indicated A on the diagram, work 16 stitches of dark gold Gobelin No. 1 in the direction indicated by the arrow. These bands of stitches should be added above and below the bands of brown wherever indicated. Next, starting at the stitch indicated B, work 16 stitches of medium gold Gobelin No. 1 in the direction indicated by the arrow. These bands of medium gold should be directly adjacent to the previously worked row of dark gold A. Finally, starting at the stitch indicated C, work 16 stitches of light gold Gobelin No. 1 in the direction of the arrow. This band of light gold should be directly adjacent to the band of medium gold B. Instructions on finishirg box tops follow.

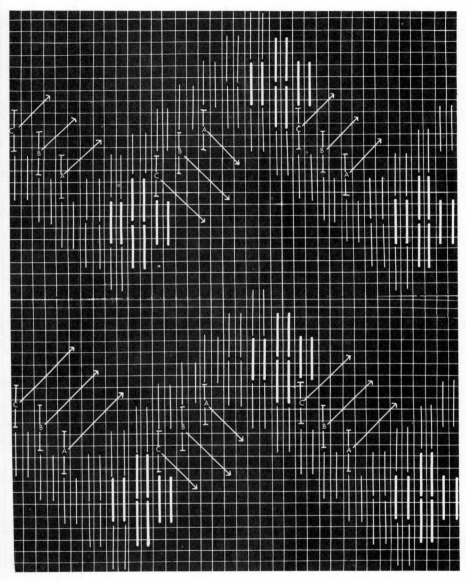

Fig. 113

INSTRUCTIONS ON FINISHING BOX TOPS

Needlepoint the design area. Block the needlepoint. Trim the canvas to within 1″ of the finished needlepoint. Using cotton batting, fill the recessed area of the wooden box. Add additional layers of cotton until the padding is about ½ to ¾ inch deep in the center of the box top. Center the finished needlepoint on the box top. Using small tacks, or staples, secure the canvas to the box top, making sure that the canvas remains centered. Tack or staple the canvas around the entire top. Trim the canvas closely to the staples or tacks. Glue upholstery trim around the box top covering all exposed canvas, ends of yarn and staples or tacks.

BOOK MARKER WITH OLD FLORENTINE DESIGN
Finished Size 1¼″ by 8″

MATERIALS

> Knitting Yarn: Light Purple—6 yards; Dark Purple—4 yards; Orange—3 yards
> No. 18 Tapestry Needle
> 10 Mesh Mono-Canvas
> Backing Material

STITCHES, COLORS AND METHOD

The long lines on the diagram indicate the dark purple Gobelin No. 1, worked over 6 threads of canvas. The short lines on the diagram indicate the orange Gobelin No. 1, worked over 2 threads of canvas. This combination of 2 short stitches followed by 2 long stitches has become known as the Old Florentine Stitch. The long and short stitches may be varied in color, as in this pattern, or the colors of the rows of the long and short stitches may be varied. Finish the long edges with light purple Whip No. 1 (use the yarn double). Finish the top and bottom ends with the light purple Turkey No. 1.

The diagram indicates the full width of the book marker, but only a portion of the length. The same sequence of colors and stitches should be continued until the book marker is the desired length. Instructions on finishing book markers follow.

67. *Extremely small and quick-to-make book markers are ideal gifts or bazaar items. They can be made from scraps of canvas and leftover yarns, each one in half an hour or so. From top to bottom: Elongated Diamond, Long and Short Flame, Old Florentine and Hungarian. Instructions for making them follow.*

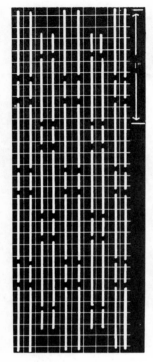

Fig. 114

BOOK MARKER—LONG AND SHORT FLAME DESIGN
Finished Size 1¼" by 7"

MATERIALS

>Knitting Yarn: Red—2 yards; Green—2 yards; Black—6 yards
>No. 20 or 22 Tapestry Needle
>12 Mesh Mono-Canvas
>Backing Material

STITCHES, COLORS AND METHOD

The long lines in the diagram indicate red Florentine No. 1, worked over 4 threads of canvas. The short lines in the diagram indicate green Florentine No. 1, worked over 2 threads of canvas. The diagram shows the full width of the book marker, but only a portion of the length. Continue working until the desired length is achieved. The triangles at the top and bottom are filled in with shorter stitches, using the same color sequence. The long edges are finished with black Whip No. 1 (yarn double). The top and bottom edges are finished with black Turkey No. 1 (yarn double). Instructions on finishing book markers follow.

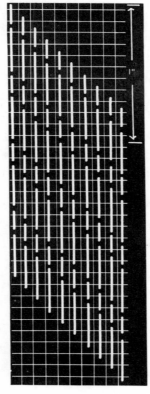

Fig. 115

155

BOOK MARKER—ELONGATED DIAMOND DESIGN
Finished Size 1¼" by 7¼"

MATERIALS

> Knitting Wool: Light Purple—1 yard; Medium Purple—3 yards;
> Dark Purple—2 yards
> No. 20 or 22 Tapestry Needle
> 12 Mesh Mono-Canvas
> Backing Material

STITCHES, COLORS AND METHOD

Florentine No. 1 is worked over 4 threads. Step 1: Beginning at the bottom of the book marker, work in dark purple until you have completed three complete diamonds. Step 2: Using medium purple, add two rows, one inside and one outside, of the motif established in the preceding step. Stitches cover 2 and 4 threads of canvas. Step 3: Fill the balance of the canvas with light purple. Stitches cover 2 and 4 threads of canvas. Work the two long edges in Whip No. 1, dark purple. Work the top and bottom in Turkey No. 1, dark purple. Instructions on finishing book markers follow.

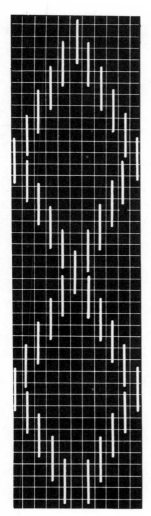

Fig. 116

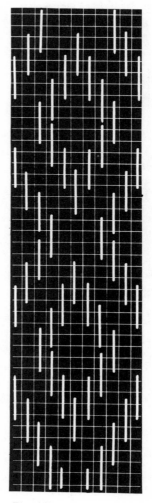

Fig. 117

157

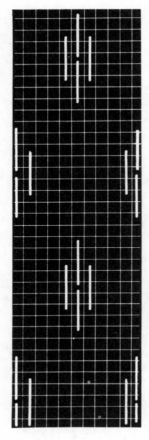

Fig. 118

BOOK MARKER—HUNGARIAN DESIGN

Finished Size 1¼" by 7"

MATERIALS

> Knitting Yarn: Light Purple—3 yards; Dark Purple—4 yards; Orange—3 yards
> No. 20 or 22 Tapestry Needle
> 12 Mesh Mono-Canvas
> Backing Material

158

The broad lines in the design indicate light purple Hungarian. The narrow lines indicate orange Hungarian. For convenience, thread a needle with each color to be used. Both colors are worked over 2 and 4 threads of canvas. Fig. 119 indicates the full width of the book marker. The length is only partially indicated—you will have to continue it, following the same color and stitch sequence, until the desired length is achieved. Work these stitches from one side to the other. Then work the next row directly under the first. It is easier to work this design in consecutive rows from the top to the bottom, rather than completing all the rows of one color, and then filling in with the other color. After the Hungarian stitches have been completed, finish the long edges with dark purple Whip No. 1. Finish the top and bottom edges with dark purple Turkey No. 1 (yarn double). Instructions on finishing book markers follow.

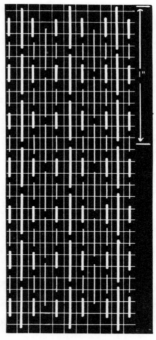

Fig. 119   Hungarian Design

INSTRUCTIONS ON FINISHING BOOK MARKERS

Needlepoint the design area. Block the needlepoint. Trim the two long edges of the canvas to within 1″ of the finished needlepoint. Turn the long edges of canvas under, leaving 2 or 3 threads of canvas exposed on the front. Using the Whip Stitch, cover the exposed edge of canvas from the top to the bottom of the Book Marker. Work the Turkey Stitch across the top and bottom of the Book Marker next tò the finished needlepoint. Trim the exposed canvas at the top and bottom to within ¾″ of the finished needlepoint. Turn the canvas to the back of the needlepoint. Cut a piece of backing material (felt, leather, cardboard) slightly narrower than the Book Marker, but the full length of the Book Marker minus the Turkey Stitch. Glue the backing material to the back of the Book Marker making sure that all exposed canvas and loose ends of yarn are covered.

BOOK COVER—GIANT DIAMOND DESIGN
Finished Size 8″ by 12″

MATERIALS

> 3-Ply Persian yarn: Purple—35 yards; White—35 yards; Pink—30 yards; Yellow—20 yards
> No. 20 or 22 Tapestry Needle
> 12 Mesh Penelope Canvas
> Address or Notebook with Removable Filler

STITCHES, COLORS AND METHOD

Step 1, Fig. 120 indicates the placement of the purple diamonds, worked with the Florentine Stitch No. 2. Each stitch covers 5 threads of canvas. Beginning at one end of the canvas, work the open diamond pattern across the entire area to be covered. Step 2, Fig. 121 shows the balance of the stitches—Florentine Stitch No. 2 worked over 4 threads of canvas. Work this band in white. It represents another open diamond pattern. This diamond fits directly inside the diamond formed by Step 1. Step 3, Fig. 122. Work a diamond pattern in pink. This open diamond pattern fits directly inside the diamond formed by Step 2. Step 4, Fig. 123. Work a diamond pattern in white. This open diamond pattern fits directly inside the diamond formed by Step 3. Step 5, Fig. 124. Fill the center of each of the diamonds with yellow. Due to the difficulty in mounting this project, it is suggested that it be turned over to a professional.

68. Shining variations on the flame pattern. The basic one is at the top left (instructions on page 165). Giant Diamonds is top right, and Flame and Diamond bottom center. In each variation, the spaces between the flames have been broken into secondary patterns.

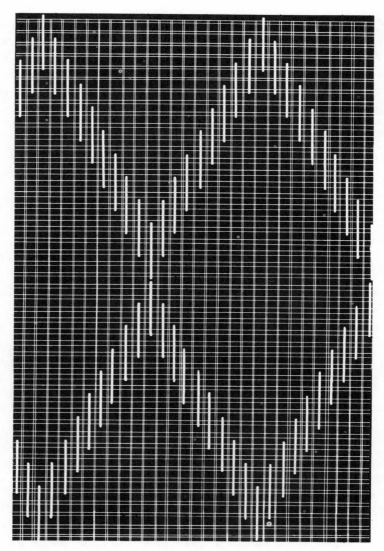

Fig. 120   *Step 1*

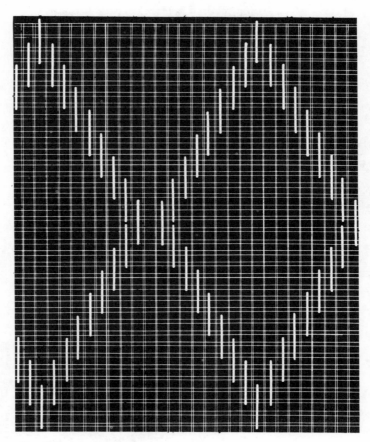

Fig. 121   Step 2

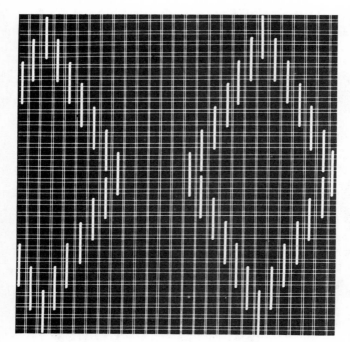

Fig. 122   Step 3

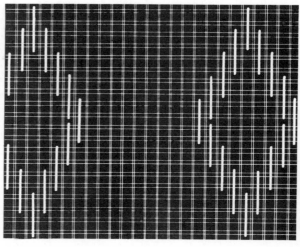

Fig. 123   Step 4

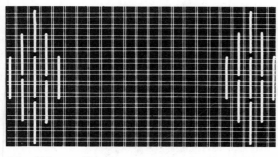

Fig. 124   Step 5

BOOK COVER—FLAME DESIGN
Finished Size 8" by 13"

MATERIALS

    4-Ply Persian Yarn: White—15 yards; Yellow—30 yards; Pink—
        25 yards; Orange—25 yards
    No. 18 Tapestry Needle
    10 Mesh Mono-Canvas
    Address or Notebook with Removable Filler

STITCHES, COLORS AND METHOD

Florentine No. 1 is the stitch used throughout. Fig. 125 shows the placement of the flame pattern. Work this pattern in white across the base of
the canvas. Each stitch will cover 5 threads of canvas. Directly above the
band of white, add three rows of yellow stitches, each row covering 5
threads of canvas. Above the yellow stitches, add two rows of orange stitches,
each row covering 5 threads of canvas. Above the orange stitches, add two
rows of pink stitches, each row covering 5 threads. Continue this sequence
of colors, starting with a single row of white again, until the entire area is
covered. The remaining points should be filled with portions of rows, retaining the same color sequence, however. Due to the difficulty in mounting
this project, it is suggested that it be turned over to a professional.

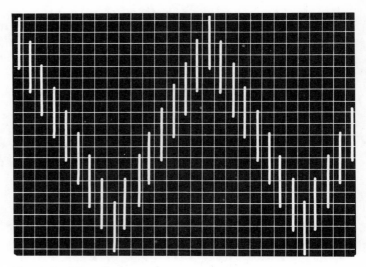

Fig. 125   Flame Design

BOOK COVER—FLAME AND DIAMOND DESIGN
Finished Size 8" by 13"

MATERIALS

    3-Ply Persian Yarn: Purple—25 yards; Pink—45 yards; White—20
      yards
    No. 20 or 22 Tapestry Needle
    12 Mesh Mono-Canvas
    Address or Notebook with Removable Filler

STITCHES, COLORS AND METHOD

Step 1, Fig. 126 indicates the placement of the purple Florentine No. 1,
worked over 4 threads of canvas. The entire area of the canvas should be
covered with this open diamond pattern. Work the diamonds so that each
point of the diamond is completed at the outside edge of the design. Step
2, Fig. 127. Inside each of the diamond patterns formed by Step 1, add one
band of white Florentine No. 1. Work the stitches above the broken line

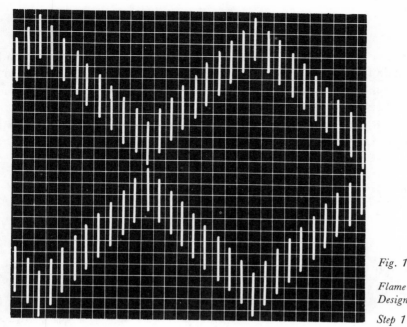

Fig. 126

Flame and Diamond Design

Step 1

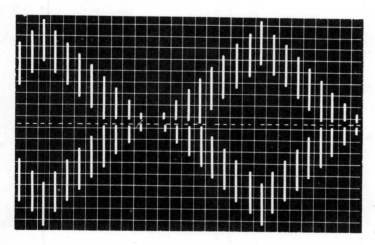

Fig. 127

Step 2

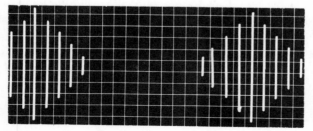

Fig. 128

Step 3

in white. They cover 1, 2, 3 and 4 threads of canvas. Below the broken line, add one band of pink Florentine Stitch No. 1. Work these over 1, 2, 3 and 4 threads of canvas. Step 3, Fig. 128. Fill in the center of the diamond with Diamond Stitch No. 1, using the pink yarn. These stitches will cover 2, 4, 6, 8 and 10 threads of canvas. Due to the difficulty in mounting this project, it is suggested that it be turned over to a professional.

Fig. 129

Chevron Design

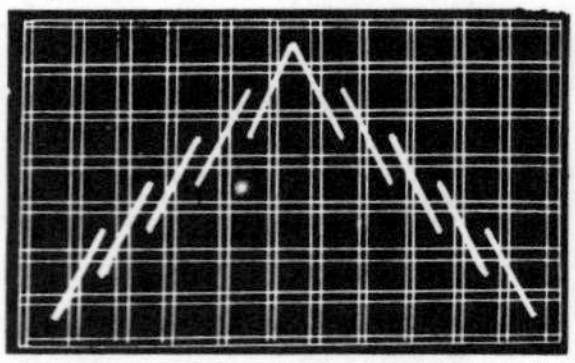

NAPKIN RING—CHEVRON DESIGN
Finished Size 2″ by 6½″

MATERIALS

> Tapestry Yarn (use double in needle): Red—8 yards; Light Pink—
> 5 yards; Dark Pink—5 yards; Salmon—5 yards
> No. 18 Tapestry Needle
> 7 Mesh Penelope Canvas
> Backing Material

STITCHES, COLORS AND METHOD

Beginning at one end of the canvas, work one red band of the Diagonal Kalem No. 2 and Reversed Diagonal Kalem No. 2 as illustrated in Fig. 129. The entire width of the ring has been diagramed, but the pattern must be continued for the required length. After working the band of red, add successive rows of dark pink, light pink and salmon. Continue this color sequence until the entire area is covered. The corners must be filled in with portions of bands, maintaining the same color sequence. Finish the long edges with red Whip No. 2. Instructions on finishing napkin rings follow.

69. *Four napkin rings. Chevron design (top); Woven Bands design (right); Candle Flame design (center); Diagonal Hungarian and Flame (lower left).*

NAPKIN RING—CANDLE FLAME DESIGN
Finished Size 3¼″ by 6″

MATERIALS

 3 Ply Persian Yarn: Gold—2 yards; Yellow—2 yards; Cream—3
  yards; White—3 yards
 Tapestry Yarn (use double in needle): Blue—24 yards
 No. 20 or 22 Tapestry Needle
 12 Mesh Mono-Canvas
 Backing Material

Florentine No. 1 is worked over 4 threads of canvas. Step 1, Fig. 130 indicates the outside band of white Florentine No. 1. There should be 3 of these motifs, placed side by side, allowing space for 3 stitches between each motif. Work Step 2, Fig. 131, in cream Florentine No. 1 and place it directly inside the white motif created in preceding step. Step 3, Fig. 132. Work in yellow Florentine No. 1 and place directly inside the cream motif created in preceding step. Work Step 4, Fig. 133, in gold Florentine No. 1 and place directly inside the yellow motif created in Step 3. Work the background in blue Florentine No. 1. Finish the long edges with blue Whip No. 1. Instructions on finishing napkin rings follow.

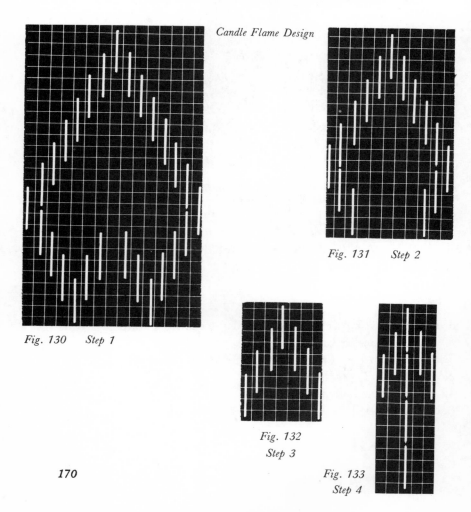

Candle Flame Design

Fig. 131   Step 2

Fig. 130   Step 1

Fig. 132
Step 3

170

Fig. 133
Step 4

NAPKIN RING—WOVEN BANDS DESIGN

Finished Size 3¾" by 5¼"
(Not Recommended for the Beginner)

MATERIALS

> Tapestry Yarn (use double in needle): Blue—12 yards; Red—6
> yards; White—10 yards
> No. 20 or 22 Tapestry Needle
> 12 Mesh Mono-Canvas
> Backing Material

STITCHES, COLORS AND METHOD

Florentine No. 1 is worked over 2 threads. The stitches indicated are bands
of red Florentine No. 1. The entire width of the ring has been diagramed,
Fig. 134, but only a portion of the length. Continue the bands until the
desired length is achieved. Start the motif in the center of the canvas and
repeat as necessary. Add parallel bands of blue Florentine No. 1 on each
side of the red band. Fill in the background with white Florentine No. 1.
Finish the long edges with white Whip No. 1. Instructions on finishing
napkin rings follow.

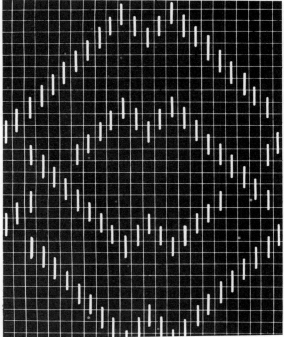

Fig. 134
Woven Bands

NAPKIN RING—DIAGONAL FLAME AND HUNGARIAN DESIGN
Finished Size 1¾" by 7"

MATERIALS

Mohair Yarn (use double in needle): White—14 yards
Knitting Yarn: Yellow—4 yards
DMC Perle No. 5: Gold—4 yards; Yellow—4 yards
No. 22 or 24 Tapestry Needle
14 Mesh Mono-Canvas
Backing Material

STITCHES, COLORS AND METHOD

Florentine No. 1 is worked over 4 threads. Hungarian is worked over 2 and 4 threads of canvas. The heavy lines in the diagram Fig. 135, indicate the placement of the Florentine No. 1, worked with the white mohair yarn. The entire width of the napkin ring has been diagramed, but the pattern must be continued for the desired length. Work the thin lines with Hungarian. Alternate the bands of color in a repeated sequence, using the yellow knitting, yellow DMC, and gold DMC yarns. Finish the long edges with Whip No. 1, using the white mohair yarn. Instructions on finishing napkin rings follow.

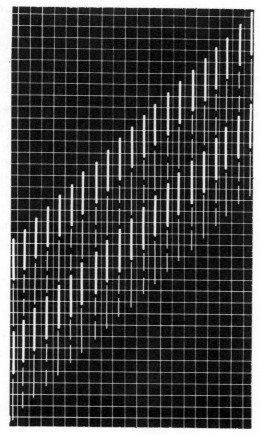

Fig. 135   Diagonal Flame and Hungarian Design

INSTRUCTIONS ON FINISHING NAPKIN RINGS

Needlepoint the design area. Block the needlepoint. Trim the canvas to within ¾" of the finished needlepoint. Turn under the raw canvas on the long edges leaving several threads of the canvas exposed. Work the Whip Stitch through the two layers of canvas covering the exposed canvas on the long edges. Trim the canvas on the short ends to within ¾" of the finished needlepoint. Turn this canvas under to the back side of the finished needlepoint. Press in place and slip stitch. Cut lining material, preferably felt, slightly narrower than the finished needlepoint. It should be slightly longer than the finished needlepoint however. With the right side exposed, slip stitch the two short ends of the finished needlepoint together. This will give you a ring, with the finished design on the outside. Slip stitch between the needlepoint stitches so that the stitches will sink between the needlepoint and be hidden. Carefully insert the lining material inside the ring. Being careful that all raw canvas and ends of yarn are covered, slip stitch through the surface of the needlepoint and secure the lining to the inside of the ring. These stitches should also be placed between the needlepoint stitches so that they will sink out of sight. The ends of the lining material may be slip stitched together, or held together with a spot of glue.

PINCUSHION OR SACHET—STRETCHED DIAMOND DESIGN
Finished Size 5" by 6¼"

MATERIALS

> Knitting Yarn (use double in needle): Black—34 yards; White—10 yards
> No. 18 Tapestry Needle
> 10 Mesh Mono-Canvas
> Backing Material
> Filler

STITCHES, COLORS AND METHOD

Florentine No. 1 and Gobelin No. 1 are worked over 4 threads of canvas. Fig. 136 indicates one-half of the motif. Work all stitches on the diagram in white. Begin at the point of the design at the right side of the canvas. When these stitches have been completed, turn the design upside down, and complete the balance of the motif. Cover the exposed canvas in black. Work the corners outside the diamond pattern in bands of black, parallel the outside band of white. Instructions on finishing pincushions or sachets follow.

70. *Pincushions or sachets are ideal gifts or bazaar items. You can make them quickly and inexpensively from scraps of canvas and leftover yarns, in sizes that suit the leftover materials. Designs clockwise from center front: Flowered Oval, Moon Eye, Beaded Diamond, Tulip, and Stretched Diamonds. Artificial flowers and beads are the accents.*

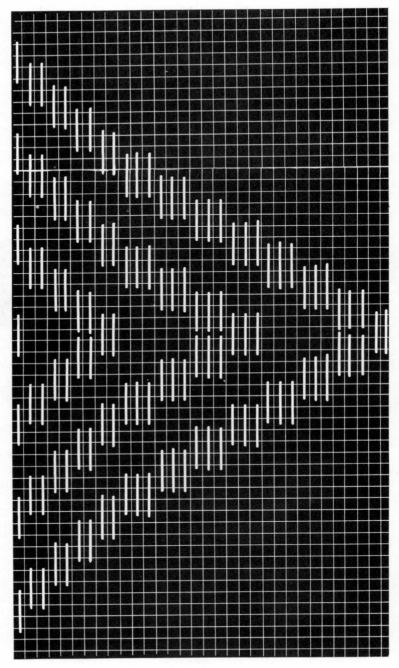

Fig. 136   Stretched Diamond Design

PINCUSHION OR SACHET—BEADED DIAMOND
Finished Size 5½" by 6½"

MATERIALS

> Knitting Wool: Light Blue—5 yards; Dark Blue—16 yards; Light
> Pink—5 yards; Red—8 yards
> 24 Blue Beads
> No. 18 Tapestry Needle
> 10 Mesh Mono-Canvas
> Backing Material
> Filler

STITCHES, COLORS AND METHOD

Florentine No. 1 and Gobelin No. 1 are worked over 4 threads. Use the
yarn double for these 2 stitches. Use the yarn double for Turkey No. 1
and single for Continental No. 1. Fig. 137 indicates the placement of two
bands of red on the canvas. Work the two bands of red in the center of
the canvas. Fill in the exposed canvas between the two bands of red with
one band of pink. Add one band of pink on the inside of the center band
of red. The balance of the center will not be filled in with needlepoint. On
the outside of the red band of stitches, add four rows of pink Continental
No. 1. Outside these four rows of pink Continental No. 1, add four rows
of red Continental No. 1. Fill in the triangular corners with light blue
Continental No. 1. Around the outside edge, add a fringe of dark blue
Turkey No. 1. In the center of the diamond, sew on 24 blue beads, covering all the exposed canvas. Instructions on finishing pincushions and sachets
follow.

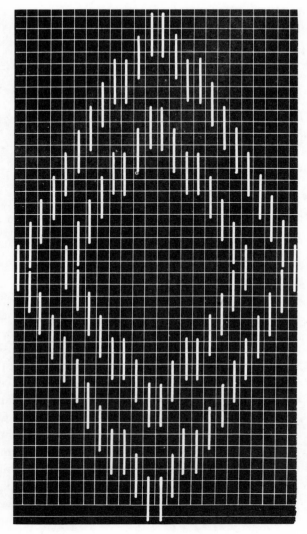

Fig. 137

PINCUSHION OR SACHET—MOON EYE DESIGN

Finished Size 5½" by 7½"
(Not Recommended for the Beginner)

MATERIALS

> Knitting Yarn (Use double in needle): Light Blue—8 yards; Dark
> Blue—7 yards; Light Purple—7 yards; Pink—30 yards
> No. 18 Tapestry Needle
> 10 Mesh Mono-Canvas
> Backing Material
> Filler

STITCHES, COLORS AND METHOD

Florentine No. 1 and Gobelin No. 1 are worked over 4 threads. Step 1,
Fig. 138. Starting from the point of the design at the right side, work this
band of light purple as shown in the diagram. This represents one-half of
the motif. When this has been completed, turn the diagram upside down
and complete the motif. Step 2, Fig. 139. Again, the diagram indicates
one-half of the motif. Work these bands in light blue; they will fit directly
inside the band of light purple completed in Step 1. Step 3, Fig. 140,
indicates the final bands of dark blue. These bands will fit between the
bands completed in Step 1 and 2. When they are completed, the entire
motif will be filled solid. Fill in the balance of the outside edges with pink,
following the basic stitch sequence established in Step 1. Instructions on
finishing pincushions or sachets follow.

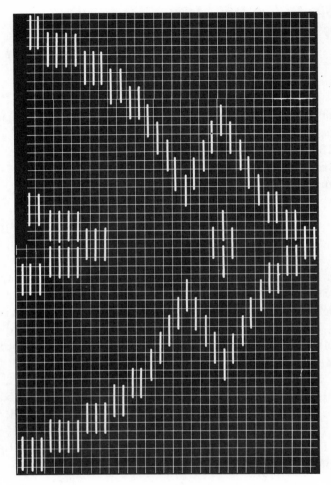

Fig. 138   Step 1

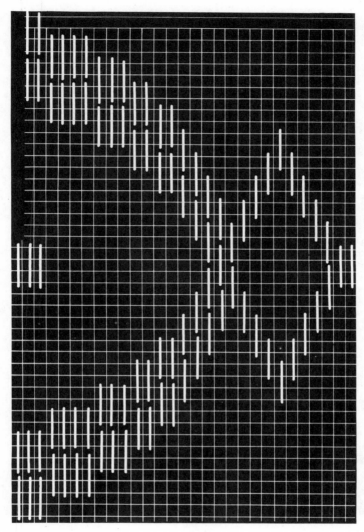

Fig. 139   Step 2

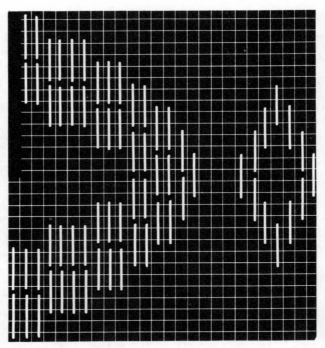

Fig. 140   Step 3

PINCUSHION OR SACHET—TULIP DESIGN
Finished Size 4½" by 6"

Materials

    3-Ply Persian Yarn: Gold—12 yards; Orange—15 yards
    Knitting Yarn: Light Rose—1 yard; Medium Rose—1 yard; Dark
      Rose—1 yard; Light Green—1 yard; Dark Green—1 yard
    No. 18 Tapestry Needle
    10 Mesh Penelope Canvas—7" by 9"
    Backing Material

This key to Fig. 141 indicates the placement of stitches and colors.

> Light Rose in Florentine No. 2
> Medium Rose in Florentine No. 2
> Dark Rose in Florentine No. 2
> Light Green in Florentine No. 2
> Dark Green in Florentine No. 2
> Background: Gold in Florentine No. 2
> Fringe: Orange in Turkey No. 2

Instructions on finishing pincushions and sachets follow.

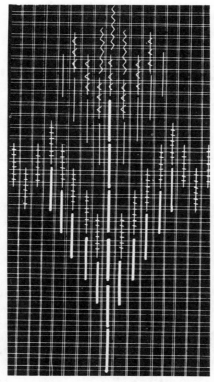

Fig. 141

PINCUSHION OR SACHET—OVAL WITH FLOWERS
Finished Size 3½" by 5½"

MATERIALS

> Knitting Yarn (Use double in needle): Blue—16 yards; Gold—12
> yards. ,
> No. 18 Tapestry Needle
> 10 Mesh Mono-Canvas
> 3 Dozen Small Artificial Flowers
> Backing Material
> Filler

STITCHES, COLORS AND METHOD

Florentine No. 1 and Gobelin No. 1 are worked over 4 threads. Fig. 142
indicates the center oval. Place this oval, worked in gold, in the center
of the canvas. Add additional bands of stitches outside this basic oval.
Alternate the colors; first gold, then blue, then gold, etc., until there are a
total of 5 bands in all. The outside corners should be filled with portions
of bands, retaining the same color sequence. Insert the flower stems through
the exposed canvas, individually, and sew securely to the back of the
needlepoint. Instructions on finishing pincushions or sachets follow.

Fig. 142   Oval Design with Flowers

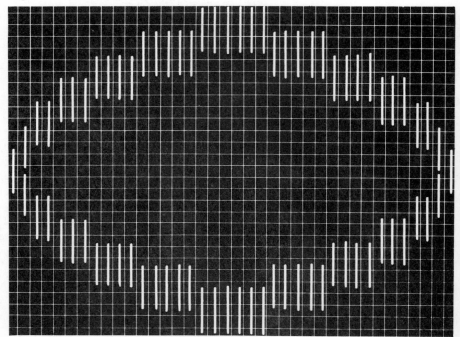

INSTRUCTIONS ON FINISHING PINCUSHIONS OR SACHETS

Follow the general directions for finishing pillows. If the needlepoint is to be used as a pincushion, fill it with cotton batting. If the needlepoint is to be used as a sachet, fill it with a sachet mixture. Because of the thickness of the needlepoint, use a lightweight backing fabric. The scent will escape more readily. It may also be advantageous to pack the finished sachet in some sachet mixture for a period of time. This way, the needlepoint will be permeated with the scent.

TRIVET—BANDED DESIGN
Finished Size 6" by 6"

MATERIALS

> Knitting Yarn (Use double in needle): Multicolored Red and Pink
> —8 yards; Black—10 yards
> No. 18 Tapestry Needle
> 7 Mesh Penelope Canvas
> Brass Trivet Frame
> Backing Material

STITCHES, COLORS AND METHOD

Brick No. 2 is worked over 2 pairs of thread. Fig. 143 indicates the beginning of the stitch placement and color placement in the center of the canvas. The heavy lines are the multicolored red and pink stitches, and the thin lines are the black stitches. Continue this progession of colors and stitches until the area is covered with 3 bands of each color. Instructions on mounting trivets follow.

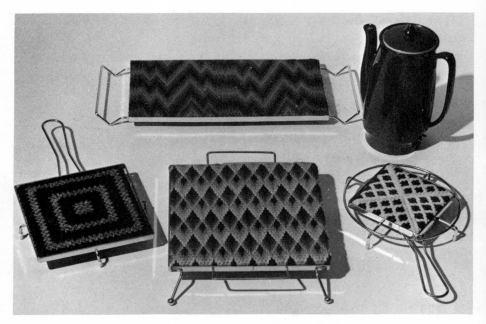

71 and Color Plate VI. Trivet bases meant for grouting and ceramic tiles hold Bargello work instead. The designs are: classic Sunrise (rear), Banded (left), Shaded Flames (center), and Grid (right).

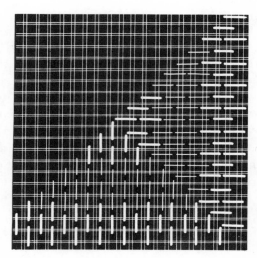

Fig. 143   Banded Design

TRIVET—GRID DESIGN

Finished Size 4½" by 4½"

MATERIALS

> Knitting Yarn (Use double in needle): Light Blue—10 yards; Dark Blue—8 yards
> No. 18 Tapestry Needle
> 7 Mesh Penelope Canvas
> Brass Trivet Stand
> Staples or Small Tacks
> Backing Material

STITCHES, COLORS AND METHOD

Brick No. 2 and Diamond No. 2 are worked over 2 pairs of thread. Fig. 144 represents a portion of the grid worked from the center out toward two sides of the trivet base. The heavy lines are light blue Brick No. 2. Continue this pattern until the entire area is covered. When half of the canvas is completed with this pattern, turn the design upside down and complete the balance of the canvas. Fill in the open centers with dark blue Diamond No. 2. Instructions on finishing trivets follow.

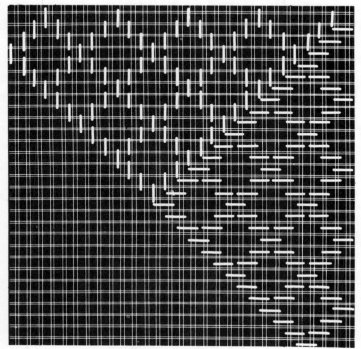

Fig. 144

TRIVET—SHADED FLAME DESIGN
Finished Size 8" by 8"

MATERIALS

4-Ply Persian Yarn: 4 shades of blue—listed Light to Dark; 1. Lightest
—9 yards; 2. 7 yards; 3. 6 yards; 4. Darkest—6 yards. (4 Shades
of Gold—Listed Light to Dark); 1. Lightest—9 yards; 2. 7 yards;
3. 6 yards; 4. Darkest—6 yards
No. 18 Tapestry Needle
10 Mesh Mono-Canvas
Brass Trivet Stand
Staples or Small Tacks
Backing Material

STITCHES, COLORS AND METHOD

Florentine No. 1 is worked over 4 threads. Step 1, Fig. 145. The heavy
lines indicate the lightest blue. The thin lines indicate the lightest gold.
Cover the entire canvas area with this pattern. Make sure that the diamonds
are completed at the top, bottom and sides so that the design will be
balanced when mounted. Step 2, Fig. 146. Directly under the point of
each diamond, add a parallel row of the next darker shade of the same
color. Step 3, Fig. 147. Directly under the band created in Step 2, add
another band of the next darker shade of the same color. Step 4, Fig. 148.
Finally, using the darkest shade, fill in the remaining area of each diamond
with the four stitches indicated. Instructions on finishing trivets follow.

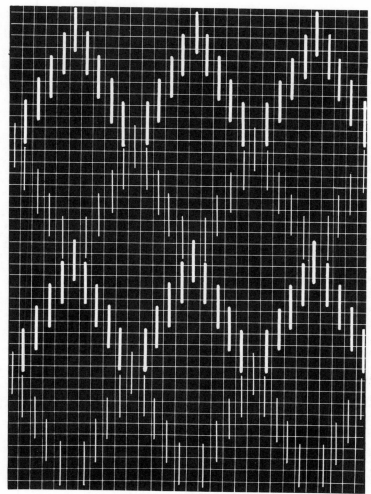

Fig. 145   Step 1

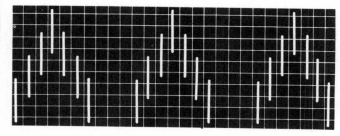

Fig. 146   Step 2

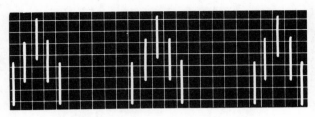

Fig. 147   Step 3

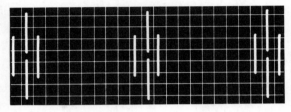

Fig. 148   Step 4

TRIVET—SUNRISE DESIGN
Finished Size 6½″ by 13″

MATERIALS

> 4-Ply Persian Yarn (16 yards of each color): Dark Purple, Medium
> Purple, Light Purple, Light Pink, Medium Pink, Dark Pink
> No. 18 Tapestry Needle
> 12 Mesh Mono-Canvas
> Trivet Base

STITCHES, COLORS AND METHOD

Florentine No. 1 is worked over 4 threads. Work the motif across the center of the canvas. One full repeat is diagrammed in Fig. 149. Work this row in dark purple. Work the balance of the rows above and below in the same stitch progression. Follow the color sequence listed under Materials, graduating the colors from dark to light back to dark again. Fill in the small spaces at the top and bottom of the trivet with portions of bands following the same color sequence. Instructions on finishing trivets follow.

190

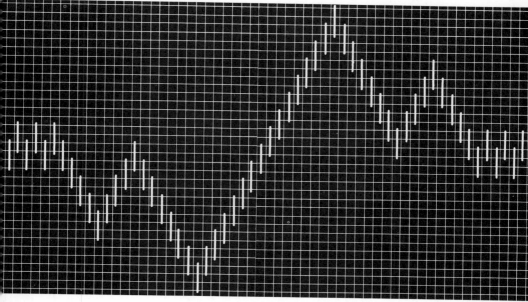

Fig. 149

INSTRUCTIONS ON FINISHING TRIVETS

Needlepoint the design area. Block the needlepoint. Remove the hardboard base from the trivet frame. Because of the thickness of the needlepoint there will have to be a clearance of approximately ⅛″ between the hardboard and the trivet frame. Trim the hardboard if necessary. Place the needlepoint, face down, on a hard working surface. Place the hardboard in the center of the needlepoint. Slip the needlepoint and hardboard, face down, in the trivet frame to see if there is clearance. Tack or staple the needlepoint to the reverse side of the hardboard. Check constantly to make sure that the hardboard is centered on the needlepoint. The tacks or staples should be about ½″ from the edge of the hardboard. After the needlepoint has been tacked or stapled down, trim the canvas to within ½″ of the tacks or staples. The back may be finished with felt or cardboard.

V Fashion Accessories

BELT—VARIED FLAME DESIGN
Finished Size 2½" by 30" plus fringe ends

MATERIALS

> Knitting Yarn: Red—15 yards; White—30 yards; Blue—15 yards
> No. 18 Tapestry Needle
> 10 Mesh Mono-Canvas
> Backing Material

STITCHES, COLORS AND METHOD

Florentine No. 1 is worked over 3, 4, 5 and 6 threads of canvas. For **Whip No. 1.** and **Turkey No. 1.** use the yarn double. Fig. 150 shows the placement of the white bands of Florentine No. 1. Bands of red and blue **Florentine No. 1** are alternated between these bands of white. For the belt design, only the stitches between *A* and *B* are used. The bands of stitches on the outside edges of the belt will have to be shortened so that the design may be accommodated to this narrow strip of canvas. If the design is to be continued, work band 1, band 2, band 3, and repeat beginning at band 1 again. Determine the length of the belt to be needlepointed. This should be 2 to 4 inches shorter than the waist size. After blocking, finish the long edges with red Whip No. 1. The short ends are finished with red, white and blue Turkey No. 1. Leave these Turkey Stitches long enough to act as ties for the belt. Stitch a long strip of lining material to the back of the belt. The edges of the lining material should be attached to the back side of the Whip. None of the raw canvas will be exposed. Instructions on finishing belts follow.

72 and Color Plate XI. Varied Flame design (top belt) is untraditional in that the stitches in each band are of different lengths, covering from 2 to 6 threads of canvas. In Reversed Points (center sash), the basic stitch sequence was established across the center. Parallel rows of stitches were added above and below. This principle applies in many Bargello patterns. At bottom, belt with Rose Design (Courtesy Mrs. Rena Sherman), the classic Bargello pattern has been worked on a small band of canvas. The pattern could be extended to cover any larger project.

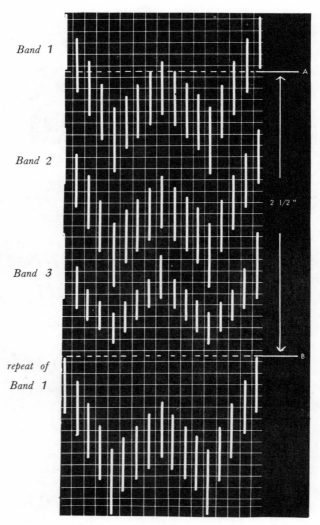

Fig. 150

BELT WITH ROSE DESIGN

Finished Size 2" by 34" plus fringe ends

MATERIALS

> 4-Ply Persian Yarn: Pink—30 yards; Purple—25 yards; Green—15 yards
> No. 18 Tapestry Needle
> 10 Mesh Mono-Canvas
> Backing Fabric

STITCHES, COLORS AND METHOD

Step 1, Fig. 151, shows the placement of the purple Gobelin No. 1. These stitches are worked over 4 threads of canvas. Work this band of stitches the entire length of the belt. The diagram indicates the full width of the belt, but only a portion of the length. Continue the same sequence of stitches until the length of the belt is achieved. This should be 2 to 4 inches shorter than the waist size. Step 2, Fig. 152 shows the placement of one band of pink Gobelin No. 1 inside each of the circles formed by Step 1. Work these stitches over 4 threads of canvas. In the open center of each of the rose patterns formed, place four Gobelin No. 1 in green. These stitches are also worked over 4 threads of canvas. Step 3, Fig. 153 shows the placement of a broken band of pink Gobelin No. 1 on the outside of each rose pattern. Work these stitches over 2 and 4 threads of canvas. Step 4, Fig. 154 indicates the placement of 6 green Gobelin No. 1 outside the pink stitches worked in Step 3. These stitches fill in the small remaining openings on the outside edges of the belt. They are worked over 2 and 4 threads of canvas. After blocking, turn under the top and bottom edges of the belt. Slip-stitch to the reverse side of the needlepoint. Work the ends of the belt with pink Turkey No. 1. These should be long enough to act as ties for the belt. Slip-stitch backing material, the same size as the belt, to the reverse side of the needlepoint. This design may be expanded to cover an indefinite area by repeating each band of purple so that the four outside Gobelin Stitches of each rose pattern touch each other. The balance of the design will be the same, except that between the bands of purple, all pink and green Gobelin Stitches will cover four threads of canvas. Instructions on finishing belts and sashes follow.

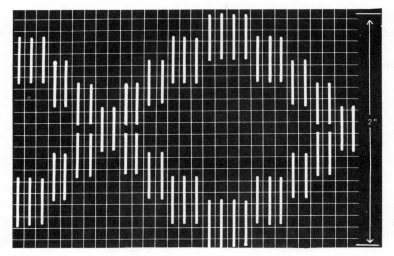

Fig. 151   Rose   Step 1

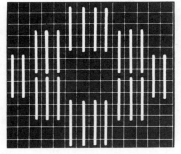

Fig. 152   Step 2

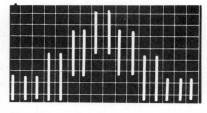

Fig. 153   Step 3

Fig. 154
Step 4

196

SASH—REVERSED POINTS DESIGN

Finished Size 4¼" by 32" plus fringe ties
(Not Recommended for the Beginner)

MATERIALS

> Paternayan Rug Yarn: Brown—35 yards; Yellow—20 yards; Gold—
> 20 yards for the sash itself; Gold—30 yards for the edges and fringe
> ends
> Rug Needle
> 5 Mesh Penelope Canvas
> Backing Material

STITCHES, COLORS AND METHOD

Florentine No. 3 is worked over 4 warp threads. Step 1, Fig. 155 indicates
the placement of a gold band. Step 2, Fig. 156 indicates the placement of a
brown band, directly below the gold band in Step 1. Step 3, Fig. 157 indicates the placement of a yellow band, directly below the brown band in
Step 2. Step 4, Fig. 158 indicates the placement of a second band of brown,
directly below the yellow band in Step 3. For a continuing pattern, repeat
the sequence from Step 1. For a belt, work one band of gold across the
center of the canvas for the desired length. This should be 2 to 4 inches
shorter than the waist size. Add parallel bands, above and below this
band, following the color sequence outlined above. Continue until the
desired width of the belt is achieved. Fill in the balance of the open spaces
with portions of bands of the colors, following the same color sequence.
After blocking, the top and bottom edges of the belt are finished with gold
Whip Stitch No. 2. Finish the ends with brown Turkey No. 2. These stitches
are not cut short, but are left long for tying purposes. The raw canvas at
the ends is turned under and slip-stitched to the reverse side of the needlepoint. Backing material, slightly narrower than the belt is slip-stitched to
the reverse side of the needlepoint. The top and bottom edges of the lining
material may be stitched to the reverse side of the Whip No. 2. Instructions
on finishing sashes follow.

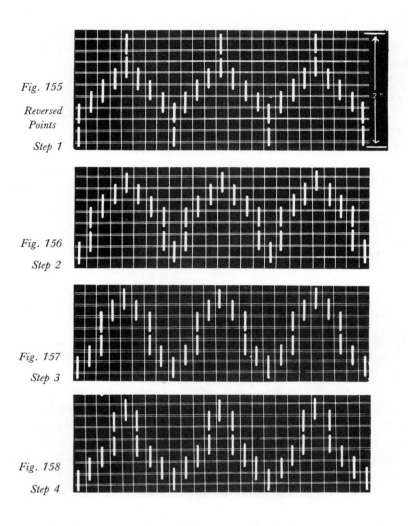

Fig. 155
Reversed
Points
Step 1

Fig. 156
Step 2

Fig. 157
Step 3

Fig. 158
Step 4

BRACELET—DIMINISHING BAND DESIGN
Finished Size 2½″ by 8″

MATERIALS

4-Ply Persian Yarn: Red—5 yards; White—5 yards; Blue—5 yards
No. 20 or 22 Tapestry Needle
12 Mesh Mono-Canvas
Backing Material

Florentine No. 1 and Gobelin No. 1 are worked over 4 threads. Fig. 159 indicates the placement of one of the bands of color across the entire width of the bracelet. This should be worked at one end of the canvas. Add parallel bands of the colors until the desired length is achieved. Fill in balance of the canvas with portions of bands, retaining the same color sequence. Instructions on finishing bracelets follow.

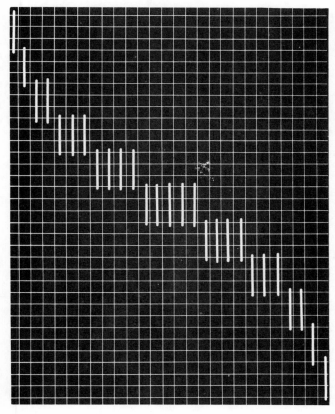

Fig. 159

73. *Designs for bracelets, worked on small bands of canvas, each could be extended indefinitely for various other projects. The designs are (top to bottom), Double Diamonds, Diamonds, Arabesque and Diminishing Bands.*

BRACELET—ARABESQUE DESIGN
Finished Size 1¾" by 7"

MATERIALS

> 4-Ply Persian Yarn: Dark Olive—2 yards; Light Olive—3 yards; Dark Blue—4 yards; Light Blue—1 yard
> No. 20 or 22 Tapestry Needle
> 12 Mesh Mono-Canvas
> Backing Material

STITCHES, COLORS AND METHOD

Florentine No. 1 and Gobelin No. 1 are worked over 4 threads. Step 1, Fig. 160. Using the dark olive, establish three complete motifs. Step 2, Fig. 161. Add two bands of dark blue on the inside and outside of the band established in Step 1. Step 3, Fig. 162. The diagram indicates the placement of the light olive. These stitches are on the outside and inside of the bands established in Step 2. Fill in the balance of the design with light blue stitches covering 4 threads of canvas each. Instructions on finishing bracelets follow.

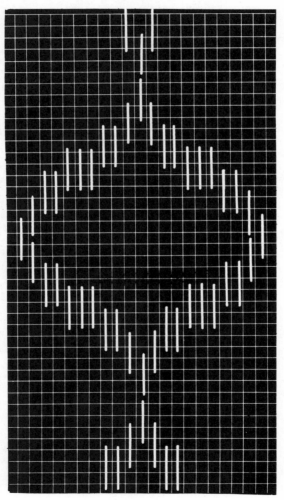

Fig. 160

Step 1

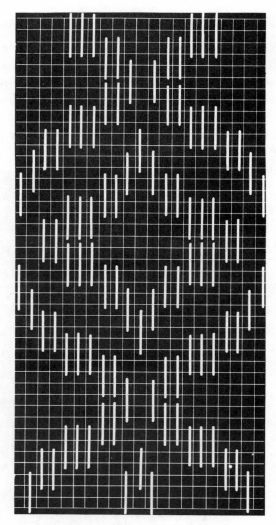

Fig. 161   Step 2

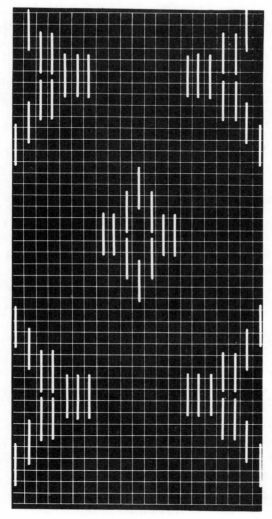

Fig. 162   Step 3

BRACELET—DOUBLE DIAMOND DESIGN
Finished Size 2¾" by 7"

MATERIALS

4-Ply Persian Yarn: Light Pink—6 yards; Dark Pink—5 yards;
   Light Orange—1 yard; Light Red—4 yards; Dark Red—5 yards
No. 20 or 22 Tapestry Needle
12 Mesh Mono-Canvas
Backing Material

STITCHES, COLORS AND METHOD .

Step 1, Fig. 163: Work this band of Florentine No. 1 in dark red, and repeat the motif 4 times. The diagram indicates slightly more than a one and one-half repeat. Stitches are worked over 4 threads of canvas in this step. Step 2, Fig. 164: Inside the band of red completed in Step 1, add this motif in light pink. The stitches are worked over 4 threads of canvas. Step 3, Fig. 165: Inside the band of light pink completed in Step 2, add this motif in dark pink. The stitches are worked over 4 threads of canvas. Step 4, Fig. 166: Inside the band of dark pink completed in Step 3, add this motif worked in orange. The stitches are worked over 4 threads of canvas. A single stitch, covering 4 threads is worked in dark red in the center of the motif. This completes the center of the motif. Step 5, Fig. 167: Add band of light red stitches, covering 2 and 4 threads of canvas to the outside of the twin diamond motif. Step 6, Fig. 168: Add short band and series of individual dark pink stitches, worked over 2 and 4 threads of canvas, to the outside of the band completed in Step 5. Step 7, Fig. 169: A cluster of light pink stitches, worked over 2 and 4 threads of canvas, is used to fill in the remainder of the canvas on the outside edge. Instructions on finishing bracelets follow.

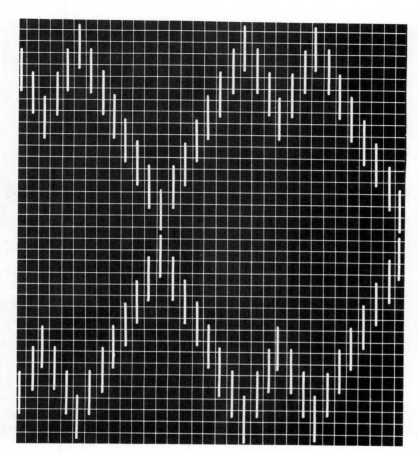

Fig. 163   Step 1

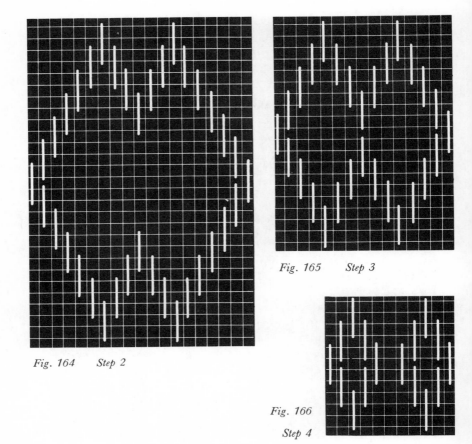

Fig. 164   Step 2

Fig. 165   Step 3

Fig. 166

Step 4

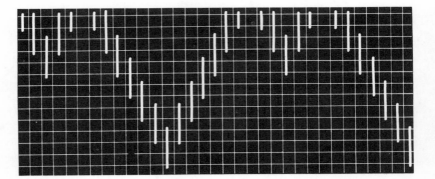

Fig. 167   Step 5

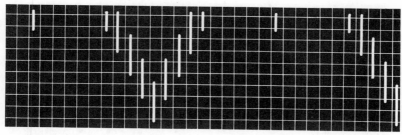

Fig. 168   Step 6

Fig. 169

Step 7

BRACELET—DIAMOND DESIGN
Finished Size 2¼″ by 7½″

MATERIALS

    4-Ply Persian Yarn: Light Blue—8 yards; Dark Blue—2 yards; Pink
    —2 yards; Purple—2 yards
    No. 20 or 22 Tapestry Needle
    12 Mesh Mono-Canvas
    Backing Material

STITCHES, COLORS AND METHOD

Hungarian is worked over 4 and 6 threads of canvas. Fig. 170 shows the
entire width of the bracelet, but only a portion of the length. Continue
the color and stitch sequence until the desired length is achieved. Band 1
is worked in purple Hungarian. Band 2 is worked in dark blue Hungarian.
Band 3 is worked in pink Hungarian. Work the background between the
three bands in light blue—Diamond No. 1, covering 2, 4, and 8 threads
of canvas. Work the two outside edges in light blue—half Diamond. No. 1,
covering 2, 3 and 5 threads of canvas. Instructions on finishing bracelets
follow.

207

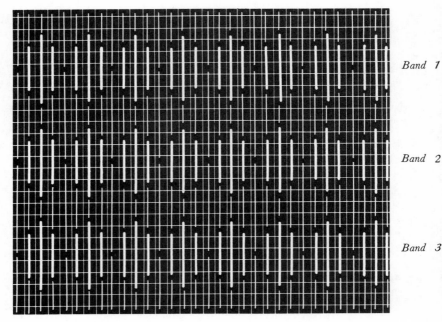

Band 1

Band 2

Band 3

Fig. 170

CHOKER—FLAME TIPS DESIGN
Finished Size 1" by 13"

Materials

    3-Ply Persian Yarn: Purple—10 yards
    Straw Yarn: Light Pink—2 yards; Dark Pink—2 yards; Purple—2
      yards
    No. 22 or 24 Tapestry Needle
    14 Mesh Mono-Canvas
    Backing Material

Stitches, Colors and Method

Florentine No. 1 is worked over 4 threads. Determine the center of the
canvas. This will be the center front of the choker or headband. Begin the
motif shown in Step 1, Fig. 171, in the center, using the light pink straw

yarn—Florentine Stitch No. 1. Continue repeating the motif until one-half of the desired length is achieved. Beginning again at the center, repeat the motifs in the reverse direction. All flames should point to the center front. The two center flame tip motifs will have one stitch, covering 4 threads of canvas between their points. Work Step 2, Fig. 172 with dark pink straw yarn. This motif is worked directly under the motif completed in Step 1. Work Step 3, Fig. 173, in purple straw yarn directly under the motif completed in Step 2. Work the background with the purple Persian yarn, using the Florentine Stitch No. 1. At either end of the choker or headband, work several Whip Stitches No. 1 with the purple Persian yarn. These should be left long to act as ties. Instructions on finishing chokers and headbands follow.

74. *Headbands or chokers. Basic Bargello techniques and designs adapted to popular fashion trends (top to bottom): Indian, Straw Diamonds, Flame Tips, and Broken Bands and Diamonds. They utilize Persian, mohair, straw and knitting yarns.*

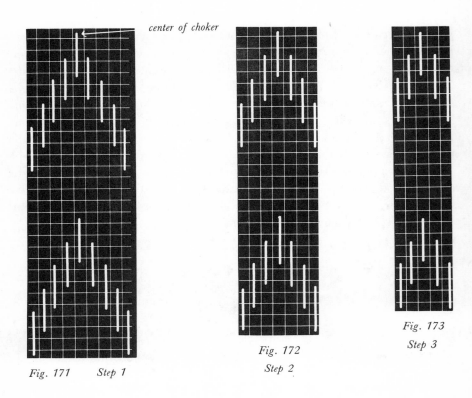

center of choker

Fig. 171   Step 1

Fig. 172
Step 2

Fig. 173
Step 3

CHOKER OR HEADBAND—STRAW DIAMONDS
Finished Size 1" by 13"

MATERIALS

    3-Ply Persian Yarn: Brown—12 yards; Orange—2 yards
    Straw Yarn (use double in needle); Orange—5 yards
    No. 20 or 22 Tapestry Needle
    12 Mesh Mono-Canvas
    Backing Material

STITCHES, COLORS AND METHOD

Diamond No. 1 and Whip No. 1 are used. Fig. 174 shows the entire width of the choker, but only a portion of the length. Continue the same sequence

210

of colors and stitches until the desired length is achieved. The heavy lines are worked with the orange straw, using the Diamond No. 1. The stitch covers 2, 4 and 6 threads of canvas. The thin line at the top and bottom of each straw diamond is worked with the orange Persian. Each one of these stitches covers 3 threads of canvas. The balance of the design is worked with the brown Persian yarn, using the Diamond No. 1. These stitches cover 4, 5 and 6 threads of canvas. At each end, attach several strands of the brown Persian yarn using the Whip No. 1. These should be left long enough to tie the choker in the back. Instructions on finishing chokers or headbands follow.

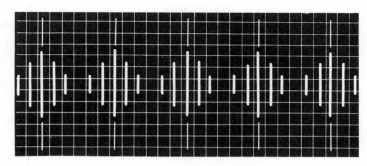

Fig. 174

CHOKER OR HEADBAND—INDIAN DESIGN
Finished Size 1″ by 10″

MATERIALS

> Knitting Yarn (use double in needle): Red—20 yards; White—15 yards
> No. 18 Tapestry Needle
> 10 Mesh Mono-Canvas
> Backing Material

STITCHES, COLORS AND METHOD

Florentine No. 1, Gobelin No. 1, Whip No. 1, Turkey No. 1, and Star are the stitches. Fig. 175 indicates one-half of the headband, with only the white stitches marked. Begin at the center of the canvas and work out to either end. After completing the white, add comparable stitches in red. The long edges are finished with the Whip No. 1. Several Turkey No. 1 stitches are added at the ends for tying purposes. A large red Star Stitch may be added to the center of the headband, directly over the white block in the middle. Instructions for finishing headbands or chokers follow.

Fig. 175

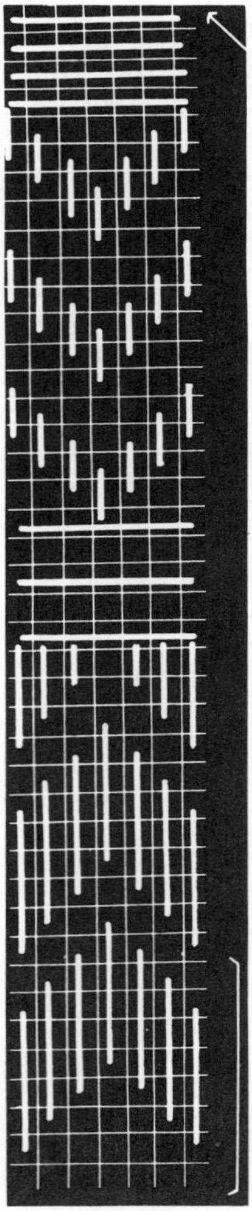

center of headband

repeat as necessary

CHOKER OR HEADBAND—BROKEN BANDS AND DIAMONDS DESIGN

Finished Size 1⅜" by 8"

MATERIALS

3-Ply Persian Yarn: Dark Olive—12 yards; Light Olive—12 yards; Blue—12 yards

Mohair Yarn: Light Blue—4 yards (use double in needle). Dark Blue—4 yards (use double in needle).

No. 22 or 24 Tapestry Needle

14 Mesh Mono-Canvas

Backing Material

STITCHES, COLORS AND METHOD

Step 1, Fig. 176. The broad line in the diagram shows the placement of the dark olive Persian yarn, worked with the Florentine No. 1 over 2 threads of canvas. The diagram shows the full width of the choker, but only a portion of the length. Continue the same sequence of stitches until the desired length is achieved. The narrow lines show the placement of the light olive Persian yarn, again worked with the Florentine No. 1. Work this band of light olive the entire length of the choker or headband, and interlock it with the dark olive previously completed. Step 2, Fig. 177. This diamond pattern will fit into the center of the open diamonds made by the two bands in Step 1. The broad line in this step indicates the light blue mohair yarn. Work these stitches over 2, 4, 6 and 4 threads of canvas. The narrow line in this step indicates the dark blue mohair yarn. Work this Diamond Stitch, also, over 2, 4, 6 and 4 threads of canvas, but in the reverse direction from the light blue mohair diamond. Step 3, Fig. 178. Add an outside border of dark blue Persian yarn, using the Diamond No. 1. Work these stitches over 2, 3, 4, 5 and 6 threads of canvas. Finish ends with dark blue Persian yarn, using the Turkey No. 1. These stitches should be left long enough to act as ties. Instructions on finishing chokers or headbands follow.

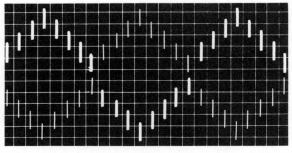

Fig. 176   Broken Bands and Diamonds Design   Step 1

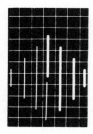

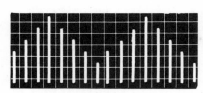

Fig. 178   Step 3

Fig. 177

Step 2

INSTRUCTIONS ON FINISHING BRACELETS, CHOKERS, HEADBANDS, BELTS AND SASHES

Needlepoint the design area. Block the needlepoint. Trim the canvas to within 1″ of the finished needlepoint for bracelets, belts and sashes; ¾″ for Chokers or Headbands. If the design specifies that the long edges be finished with the Whip Stitch, turn under the raw canvas leaving several threads of canvas exposed. Work the Whip Stitch through the two layers of canvas covering the exposed canvas on the long edges. Work the Turkey Stitch across the short ends of the needlepoint, next to the finished needlepoint. No canvas should be left exposed between the Turkey stitch and the finished needlepoint itself. These ends should be left long enough for tying purposes. Trim the canvas under the Turkey stitch to within 1″ of the finished needlepoint. Turn the raw canvas to the back and slip-stitch to the back of the finished needlepoint. Cut backing material, preferably felt, slightly narrower than the finished piece of needlepoint. The backing material should be as long as the finished needlepoint minus the Turkey

Stitch. Slip-stitch the backing material to the back of the needlepoint, covering all exposed canvas and yarn ends. The backing material may be attached to the back side of the Whip Stitch and will not be seen from the face of the needlepoint. If the Whip stitch is not used to finish the long ends of needlepoint, carefully turn under the canvas on all sides. Slip-stitch to the back of the finished needlepoint. Slip-stitch the backing material to the edges of the finished canvas. Great care must be exercised that the stitches and backing material do not show at the ends of the needlepoint. Buckles or rings may be attached to the ends of belts or sashes, intead of using a Whip stitch for tying. Bracelets may be secured with snaps or hooks and eyes attached to the ends of the bracelet.

BAG—SCALLOP DESIGN
Finished Size 5½" by 6"

MATERIALS

> 3-Ply Persian Yarn (20 yards of each shade): Light Blue, Medium Blue, Dark Blue, Light Olive, Medium Olive, Dark Olive
> No. 20 or 22 Tapestry Needle
> 12 Mesh Mono-Canvas
> Lining Material
> Trim

STITCHES, COLORS AND METHOD

Gobelin No. 1 is worked over 4 threads. Starting at the bottom of the canvas, work Scallop No. 1, Fig. 179, in light blue Gobelin Stitch No. 1 Scallop No. 2, Fig. 179, is worked in the same stitch, but in light olive. Continue this sequence until 5½ inches of canvas has been covered. A second row of scallops is added above the first, however, scallop no. 1 is worked in medium blue, and scallop no. 2 is worked in medium olive. The third row is worked in dark blue and dark olive. The entire canvas may be worked continuing this sequence of colors, or the three rows of scallops may be alternated. That is, three rows of green may be worked above three rows of blue, and three rows of blue may be worked above the three rows of green. The scallop pattern is continued until the area covered measures

$5\frac{1}{2}''$ by $15''$. After blocking the canvas, with right sides of the finished needlepoint together, turn up 6 inches of the canvas. Turn back the selvage edge of the canvas so that it is on the back side of the canvas. Stitch the two sides of the canvas together. Slip-stitch the selvage edge of the canvas to the back side of the needlepoint. Turn this pouch inside out. Cut a piece of lining material $6''$ by $15''$. Turn up 6 inches of the lining material on itself. Stitch the sides to form a pouch similar to the needlepoint pouch. Turn under the remaining edges of raw needlepoint on the flap. Slip the lining pouch down inside the needlepoint pouch. Slip-stitch the edges of the lining pouch to the edges of the needlepoint. Trim edges of flap with braid. A long chain may be slipped under the flap and stitched in place.

Fig. 179

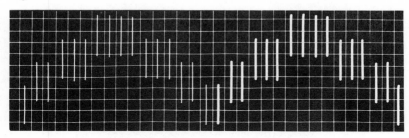

Scallop Design Scallop No. 1   Scallop No. 2

SUPER NECKLACE
Finished Size 12" by 13"

MATERIALS

 6-Ply Persian Yarn: Pink—15 yards; Dark Blue—10 yards; Light
  Blue—12 yards; Gold—15 yards; Red—10 yards; Yellow—10 yards
 5 Mesh Penelope Canvas
 Rug Needle
 Backing Material
 Hooks and Eyes

STITCHES, COLORS AND METHOD

Kalem and Reversed Kalem are the stitches. The color key to Fig. 180 is
(1) Pink; (2) Dark Blue; (3) Light Blue; (4) Gold; (5) Red; (6) Yellow. Needlepoint the entire necklace. Block canvas. Trim raw canvas to
within ¾ inch of finished needlepoint. Carefully turn under raw canvas
and baste to reverse side of needlepoint. Cut lining fabric and slip-stitch
through surface of needlepoint, between stitches, as close as possible to edge.
Press. Attach hooks and eyes to necklace in back.

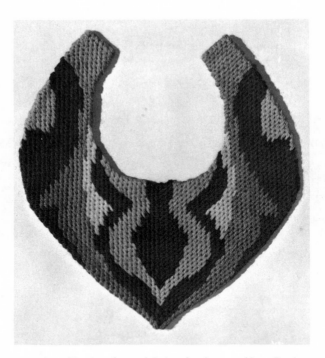

76. *An unusual combination of materials in a handsome necklace. Persian yarns, used 6-ply, have been worked on 5 mesh Penelope canvas, a size canvas usually reserved for rug yarns or other bulky yarns.*

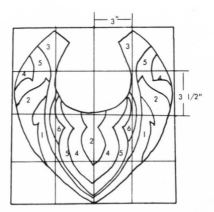

Fig. 180

EYEGLASS CASE—PLASTIC DIAMOND DESIGN

Finished Size 3½" by 7"

MATERIALS

3-Ply Persian Yarn: Dark Gold—6 yards; Medium Gold—8 yards;
   Light Gold—4 yards
25 Plastic Diamonds
No. 20 or 22 Tapestry Needle
12 Mesh Mono-Canvas
Lining Material
Trim (Optional)

STITCHES, COLORS AND METHOD

Florentine No. 1 is worked over 4 threads. Step 1, Fig. 181. Using the
dark gold in Florentine Stitch No. 1 establish this open diamond pattern
over the entire area of the canvas. You will note that the pattern produces
a row of small diamonds, followed by a row of large diamonds. This
pattern is continued. Step 2, Fig. 182. Inside the large diamonds formed
by Step 1, work a row of medium gold using the Florentine Stitch No. 1.
Step 3, Fig. 183. Inside the diamonds formed by Step 2, work 4 light gold
stitches in Florentine No. 1. This will fill the large diamonds. Sew the
plastic diamonds, or other suitable decorations, inside the small diamonds
which have not been filled in with needlepoint. Instructions on finishing
eyeglass cases follow.

77. *Eyeglass cases. Points and Waves (foreground) has been worked in Persian yarns on a small mesh canvas. In Plastic Diamond (left) an imitation gem is sewn into the middle of the pattern. Large and Small Points (right) owes its furry appearance to the exclusive use of mohair yarns.*

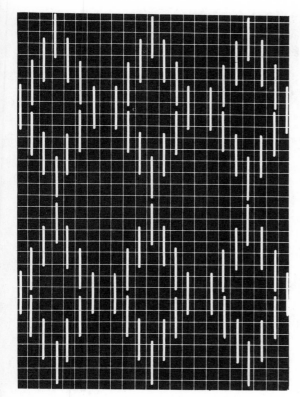

Fig. 181   Step 1

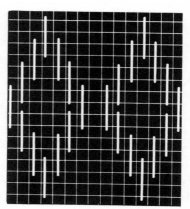

Fig. 182   Step 2

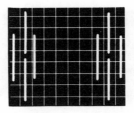

Fig. 183   Step 3

EYEGLASS CASE—LARGE AND SMALL POINTS DESIGN
Finished Size 3½" by 6½"

MATERIALS

Mohair Yarn (use double in the needle): 4 shades of blue—6 yards
of each shade
No. 20 or 22 Tapestry Needle
12 Mesh Mono-Canvas
Lining Material
Trim (Optional)

STITCHES, COLORS AND METHOD

Florentine No. 1 is worked over 4 threads. Fig. 184 indicates one band of color worked across the entire width of the top of the eyeglass case. After this pattern has been established, add additional bands directly below the first band, following the same stitch sequence. The sequence of colors in this eyeglass case range from light at the top to dark at the bottom. Repeat the colors until the bottom of the case is reached. Fill in the balance of the exposed canvas with portions of bands, following the same sequence of colors. After the project has been blocked and mounted, you may wish to brush the mohair to free the ends which have become imprisoned in the canvas and in adjoining stitches. This will produce a fuzzy and typically mohair look. Instructions on finishing eyeglass cases follow.

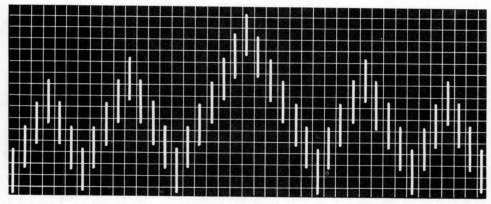

Fig. 184

EYEGLASS CASE—POINTS AND WAVES DESIGN
Finished Size 4" by 6½"

MATERIALS

> 3-Ply Persian Yarn: Light Green—3 yards; Medium Green—3 yards;
> Dark Green—3 yards; Light Blue—3 yards; Medium Blue—3
> yards; Dark Blue—3 yards
> No. 20 or 22 Tapestry Needle
> 12 Mesh Mono-Canvas
> Lining Material
> Trim (Optional)

STITCHES, COLORS AND METHOD

Florentine No. 1 is worked over 4 threads. Fig. 185 indicates the placement of one band of light green across the entire eyeglass case. Work this band across the top of the canvas. Add additional bands, following the same stitch pattern, below this band. The color sequence should be light green, light blue, medium green, medium blue, dark green and, finally, dark blue. Repeat this sequence of colors until the entire area is covered. The exposed portions of canvas should be filled in with portions of bands, following the same sequence of colors. Of course, the color sequence may be varied from the above formula. However, whenever a color sequence is established, it should be adhered to until the project is completed. Instructions on finishing eyeglass cases follow.

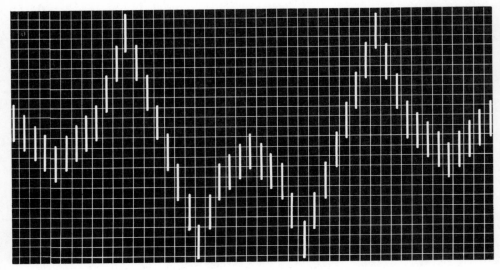

Fig. 185

INSTRUCTIONS ON FINISHING EYEGLASS CASES

Needlepoint the design area. Block the needlepoint. Trim the canvas to within ½" of the finished needlepoint. Turn the raw canvas to the reverse side of the needlepoint. Slip-stitch in place. Carefully press the canvas to the reverse side of the needlepoint. Cut two pieces of lining material, preferably felt, ⅛" smaller than the finished needlepoint. Attach one piece of felt to the reverse side of the top of one of the pieces of needlepoint. Repeat with the other piece of felt. Lay the two pieces of felt together, with the right side of the needlepoint on the outside. Using a small needle and fine thread, stitch through the two layers of needlepoint and two layers of felt on both sides of the eyeglass case, and across the bottom. Place these stitches between the needlepoint stitches so that they sink between the needlepoint stitches and become invisible. If trim is desired, secure it along

224

the sides and bottom of the eyeglass case to cover the edges. Great care must be taken when the canvas is turned under so that no raw canvas is left exposed.

TANK TOP—ST. VALENTINE DESIGN
Finished Man's Size 36"
(Not Recommended for the Beginner)

MATERIALS

> Paternayan Rug Yarn: 5 shades of Blue (Listed Light to Dark) This will finish front only. 1. Light—10 yards; 2. 35 yards; 3. 45 yards; 4. 55 yards; 5. Dark—50 yards. Also Light Green—30 yards; Medium Green—15 yards; Dark Green—10 yards
> Rug Needle
> 5 Mesh Penelope Canvas
> Lining Material
> Trim (Optional)

STITCHES, COLORS AND METHOD

Florentine No. 3 and Gobelin No. 3 are worked over 2 pairs of warp thread. Step 1, Fig. 186, indicates one complete heart motif, and the beginning of the motif to the top, bottom and two sides. This motif should be worked across the entire canvas, starting at the bottom of the project. This outline of the heart is worked in the dark blue. Steps 2 through 5, Figs. 187-190, indicate the placement of bands of blue inside each heart motif. Each succeeding band is one shade lighter, until in Step 5, the lightest shade of blue is used. The diamond patterns in between the hearts are worked in green. Step 6, Fig. 191, is worked in light green and will be worked directly adjacent to the dark blue outline of each heart. Step 7, Fig. 192, is worked in medium green and is worked directly inside Step 6. Finally, Step 8, Fig. 193, is worked in the center of each diamond, using the dark green. Instructions on finishing tank tops follow.

78 and Color Plate IX. This tank top with St. Valentine design, worked with Paternayan rug yarns on rug canvas, is an example of the application of traditional needlepoint to a contemporary fashion, and the use of unorthodox materials to achieve an interesting effect. It has the texture and feeling of a very heavy wool sweater. This pattern
would be particularly effective for an area rug.

Fig. 186   Step 1

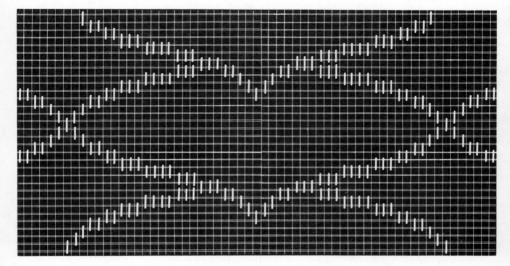

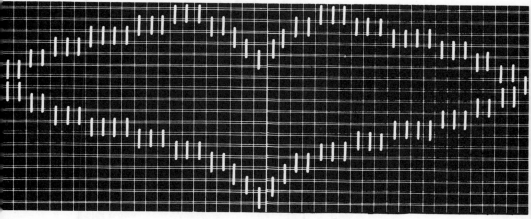

Fig. 187   *Step 2*

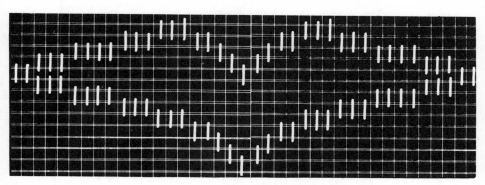

Fig. 188   *Step 3*

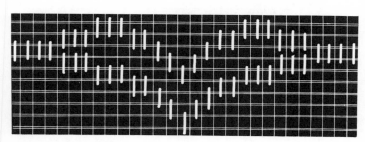

Fig. 189   *Step 4*

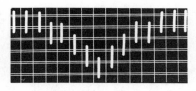

Fig. 190   Step 5

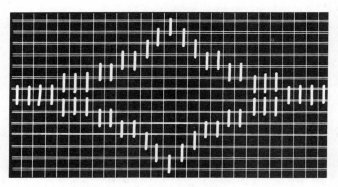

Fig. 191   Step 6

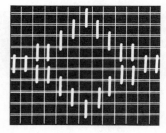

Fig. 192   Step 7

Fig. 193
Step 8

Opposite 79. This paisley vest has the unusual combination of Persian yarns worked on rug canvas. The Persian yarn was used double, that is, 6 ply on the canvas, to give a softer effect than would have been achieved with rug yarns. Although wildly exuberant, the pattern has a timeless quality about it whcih will survive the passing fashion fads.

VEST—PAISLEY DESIGN
Finished Size 10" by 24"

MATERIALS

6-Ply Persian Yarn: Red—40 yards; Gold—15 yards; Brown—20 yards; Blue—20 yards; Olive—30 yards; Green—30 yards; Yellow —20 yards; Gray—12 yards
5 Mesh Penelope Canvas
Rug Needle
Lining Material
Trim

STITCHES, COLORS AND METHOD

Encroaching Oblique and Reversed Encroaching Oblique are used. The color key to Fig. 194 is (1) Red; (2) Gold; (3) Brown; (4) Blue; (5) Olive; (6) Green; (7) Yellow; (8) Gray. Instructions on finishing vests follow.

2 1/2"

Fig. 194

6"

VEST—PEACOCK'S EYE DESIGN

Finished Man's Size 36"
(Not Recommended for the Beginner)

MATERIALS

> Paternayan Rug Yarn (This yarn will finish front only): Light Yellow—40 yards; Medium Yellow—32 yards; Dark Yellow—32 yards; Light Gold—28 yards; Dark Gold—28 yards; Light Blue—28 yards; Light Turquoise—18 yards; Medium Blue—16 yards; Dark Turquoise—8 yards; Dark Blue—6 yards; Black—6 yards
> Rug Needle
> 5 Mesh Penelope Canvas
> Lining
> Trim (Optional)

STITCHES, COLORS AND METHOD

Florentine No. 3 is worked over 2 pairs of warp thread. Step 1, Fig. 195, indicates one complete design worked in light yellow, and the beginning of

230

repeats at the top, bottom and two sides. This pattern should be worked across the entire area. Steps 2 through 11, Figs. 196-205, indicate the placement of additional bands within each pattern. Each band is placed directly under the preceding band until the small eye is completed in Step 11 at each base. The color sequence for the vest continues: Step 2—Medium Yellow. Step 3—Dark Yellow. Step 4—Light Gold. Step 5—Dark Gold. Step 6—Light Blue. Step 7—Light Turquoise. Step 8—Medium Blue. Step 9—Dark Turquoise. Step 10—Dark Blue. Step 11—Black. Instructions on finishing vests follow.

80 and Color Plate XV. Vest with Peacock's Eye design. This pattern demonstrates the effectiveness of combining two contrasting colors within the same pattern gradation. A pattern such as this, with diminishing rows of stitches, would have been effective worked in progressively darker shades of a single color. However, in this design, the introduction of the dark blue serves to accent and intensify the curved and diminishing line of the design.

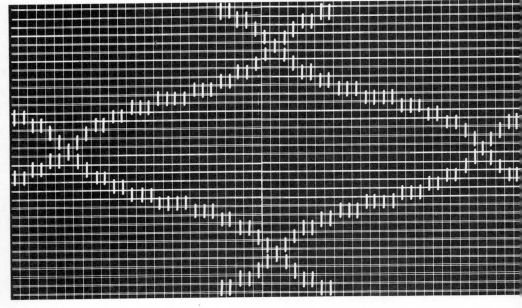

Fig. 195   *Step 1*

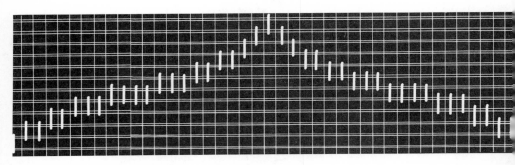

Fig. 196   *Step 2*

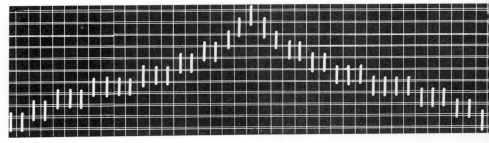

Fig. 197   *Step 3*

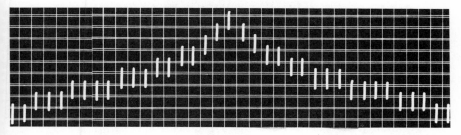

Fig. 198   Step 4

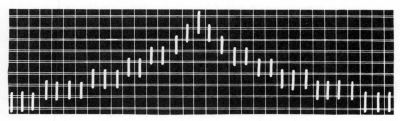

Fig. 199   Step 5

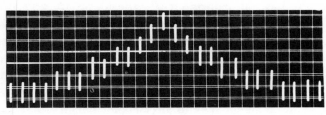

Fig. 200   Step 6

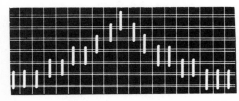

Fig. 201   Step 7

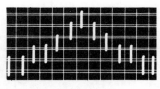

Fig. 202   Step 8

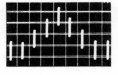

Fig. 203   Step 9

Fig. 204

Step 10

Fig. 205

Step 11

INSTRUCTIONS ON FINISHING TANK TOPS AND VESTS

Secure a commercial pattern of the desired project, or have a pattern made from a favorite garment. The pattern should be simple, free from darts, gathers, buttons, etc., and should fit properly. If in doubt, make a sample using muslin before investing the time and money in the needlepoint project. Trace the design to be used on the canvas, on a piece of paper larger than the pattern design. Lay the canvas on the traced design, and trace the design onto the canvas. (See Chapter on Altering Designs) Make sure that the design is centered on the pattern, and if the pattern consists of matching pieces, that the design balances on both sides. Needlepoint the design area. Block the finished needlepoint. Follow the pattern instructions on assembling and lining the garments. Lining materials should be lightweight because of the inherent bulk of needlepoint design. Most garments may be finished by a professional.

Supplies

All of the materials in this book will be readily available at needlecraft shops . . . and don't overlook the needlecraft shop in large department stores. If you should have difficulty finding special materials, please contact the authors in care of the publishers, Hearthside Press Inc., 445 Northern Boulevard, Great Neck, New York 11021, enclosing a stamped, self-addressed envelope, for information.

INDEX